TEMPLE BALSALL

From Hospitallers to a Caring Community
1322 to Modern Times

TEMPLE BALSALL

From Hospitallers to a Caring Community
1322 to Modern Times

Eileen Gooder

Phillimore

1999

Published by
PHILLIMORE & CO. LTD.
Shopwyke Manor Barn, Chichester, West Sussex

ISBN 1 86077 102 5

Printed and bound in Great Britain by
BOOKCRAFT LTD.
Midsomer Norton

Dedicated
to all the many lovers
of
Temple Balsall

What is it about this place that so captures the imagination? It is the vein of goodness that runs through more than eight hundred years of history; the Crusades, flawed, but originating in noble aspirations; the 17th-century foundation of the almshouses for poor old women and the school for poor boys and later poor girls; the modern haven for aging persons where they can live out a peaceful life in loving care; the church with its hundreds of years of prayer; the little country school where bonny children make a wholesome start in life; a cheerful goodness is in the very air of this unique and lovely spot.

Contents

Appendices

List of Illustrations

Acknowledgements

I am indebted to many people for their encouragement, support and active help. They are: Tom Arkell, Alan and Elsie Birch, Geoffrey and Eileen Burman, Jean Carter, Rod Crossley, Valerie Goode, Richard Lawton, Jeanne Moss, Derek Robinson, Peter Searby, Roger Stone, David Warren, Rev. R. Watson Williams, Fred West, Frances Wilmot, Pat Watts and her family, Kathy Williams (née Watts). My sincere thanks to them all.

My debt is especially great to David and Sheila Sheppard for their help in all departments of the work, including research. Without this help, the book would never have been completed.

A special vote of thanks goes to my publishers for their great care in the production of this book, particularly in the case of the illustrations; from these (and in some cases only substandard specimens were available) they have succeeded in producing clear and telling images.

I am grateful to the following for allowing me to reproduce copyright material: D.N. Booth for the drawing of Temple Balsall farm wheel from *Warwickshire Watermills*; Geoffrey Burman for the letter about Mary Powner; Caroline Jones for photographs of Balsall Street School from *Balsall Street School: The First 75 Years*; the County Archivist for numerous quotations from Temple Balsall Mss deposited at the County Record Office and reproduction of portraits from *The Italian Biography of Sir Robert Dudley* (Anon.); C.R. Humphery-Smith, F.S.A., illustrations of the Hospital of St John in Jerusalem from his biography *Hugh Revel* (1994); Oxford University Press for the illustration of the timber-framed house-building from L.F. Salzman's *Building in England* (1940); the Royal Commission for Historic Monuments for the Schematic Ground-Floor Plan of the Old Hall, Temple Balsall; and Pam Taylor for her photographs of the East Window of St Mary's Church, Temple Balsall.

Every endeavour has been made to secure the appropriate copyright permissions.

Prologue

The Knights of St John
The Foundation of the Order

There are several versions of the origins of the Hospitallers, all regarded by some historians as apocryphal.[1] But the account given by William, Archbishop of Tyre, writing between 1170 and 1182, is generally accepted as being as near to the truth as we are likely to get.[2]

It runs as follows: Italian merchants visiting the holy places in Jerusalem, and having no lodgings there, were given land next to the church of the Holy Sepulchre, where they built a monastery dedicated to the Virgin Mary; they settled an Italian abbot and monk there, and the monastery became known as St Mary of the Latins. In the middle of the 11th century there was a great increase of pilgrimages and, to provide for female pilgrims, a daughter convent, dedicated to St Mary Magdalene, was built, followed by a hospice, dedicated to St John (probably the Baptist). These last two were certainly functioning before the first Crusade in 1095. The hospice or hospital seems to have been treated as a separate organisation from about 1103, receiving gifts in its own right. The Pope established the Hospitallers as an independent Order in 1113 (fifteen years before the Rule of the Templars was sanctioned), and by that date they had a number of dependent hospices on the route from western Europe to the Near East. They were now an international religious Order, like the Templars answerable only to the Pope.

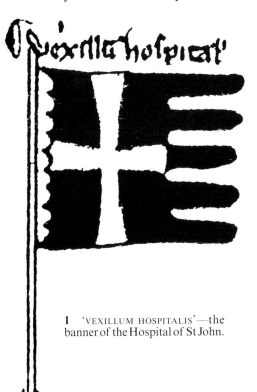

1 'VEXILLUM HOSPITALIS'—the banner of the Hospital of St John.

1

2 The banners of the Hospitallers (left) and Templars (right), with above the escutcheons of nobles overthrown at the defeat at Gaza in 1239. Extract drawn from BL Royal Ms 14 C vii, f.130v.

The organisation of the Hospitallers was similar in many ways to that of the Templars. There were three grades of Brothers, the knights, the priests, and the serving brothers (the sergeants). The last group were divided into sergeants-at-arms and sergeants-of-office, according to their function.[3] All were supposed to attend the customary monastic hours (the seven canonical hours), and were expected to say 150 paternosters each day.[4]

By the strict letter of their Rule they were to eat only twice a day, which seems to have been observed, and their houses strictly were only supposed to supply bread and water, but it is obvious that this was only adhered to as a punishment, for by an order of 1206 it was laid down that the food and drink should be good enough to be tolerated by all brothers if the house could afford it. Ordinances about fasting were many and varied, but there were so many dispensations and absolutions that it is abundantly clear that the brethren fared well at the table, with meat, fish, wheaten bread, beer and 'other necessaries of the kitchen' freely available.[5] It is very likely that the hospitality which most of their major houses offered to travellers (and indeed were bound to offer by their Rule and many of their charters) encouraged the provision of a palatable and generous diet.[6]

The brothers were supposed to eat in silence and good order, but it is clear that meal-times sometimes became rowdy, the brethren beating the paid serving-men and pelting them with bread and wine.[7] A further departure from austerity was the provision of pittances, special allowances on special occasions (a practice common in many medieval monasteries), and even sometimes to brethren undergoing punishment.[8]

The Rule decreed that their dress should be humble, no bright colours, no fur; all should wear a cross embroidered on the breast of their mantles and on their caps. At first the knights were supposed to be distinguished by the black mantle, but after 1278 all were allowed to wear the black though not all did so. By 1206 their issue of clothing was generous, including three shirts, three pairs of breeches, a *cotta* (sleeveless tunic), a *garnache* (buttoned jacket) with hood, and two mantles, one lined with fur. The 'no-fur' regulation was forgotten, and perhaps it was impractical in cold weather (both the Hospitallers and the Templars were mindful of keeping the troops in fighting order).

3 The Hospital of St John in Jerusalem from a 13th-century manuscript in the Escorial. The best sheets and silver vessels were used for the care of the sick. (From C. Humphery-Smith, *Hugh Revel: Master of the Hospital of St John of Jerusalem 1258-1277*, 1994. Reproduced by permission.)

They had hose of linen and wool, and shoes described as 'conventual'. At night they could wear boots, perhaps as being warmer.

The provision of clothing became a burden on the Order's finances, and in 1263 it was decreed that new brothers should provide their own, and in 1302, that they were to be issued with money to buy their own clothes. They were also issued with a small sum as pocket-money, and this was spent by some on more glamourous clothing, bright colours, gold and silver thread, embroidered kerchiefs and turbans, and a more fashionable cut for the regulation items.[9]

From the foregoing, it is clear that the Hospitallers had diverged from the austerity of earlier years and, after the fall of the Templars, their funds augmented with those of their former rivals, in 1343 (following the near-bankruptcy of the Order in 1328) Pope Clement VI wrote to the Master:

> Popular and clergy opinion is that you profit almost nothing from the innumerable goods of the Hospital, overseas and elsewhere, except that the Hospitallers themselves ride great and beautiful horses, are at leisure with delicious food, ostentatious dress, and use gold and silver vessels and other precious ornaments; they keep and nurture birds [?falcons] and hunting dogs, amass innumerable sums of money and bestow alms only rarely and moderately.

The Pope hinted at creating another military order instead of the Hospitallers, but of course this came to nothing.[10]

Nevertheless, their system of punishments, many of which were similar to those imposed by the Templars, still held sway; for minor offences such as rowdiness, ill behaviour in church, or minor insubordination, the offender would be beaten in church, then must exchange the kiss of peace with his superior; he must eat on the ground without a napkin for a week (with bread and water only for two of the days). A more serious punishment lasted for 40 days and the Brother would be stripped naked for the beating in church; violence against another Brother merited this. More serious still was the 'loss of habit', 'loss of the company of the house' and flogging with hard rods. It was possible to recover from this expulsion after a period, at the discretion of the Master. Permanent expulsion was reserved for those who were heretics, for sodomites or those who bore false witness, for those who fled from battle or deserted to the Saracens. But the severity of some of the lighter punishments could be mitigated by the Master if he thought the health of the offender might suffer, and he could order pittances at his discretion for those deprived of wine.

All in all, life for the Hospitallers was far from unbearable, and did not share the austerity and asceticism of some contemporary religious orders. Above all, it was adaptable.[11]

Sisters of St John

In the 11th century, near the great Hospital in Jerusalem, was a St John's hospice for women pilgrims, which in the next century became the independent convent of St Mary Major. Women must have served in the Hospital itself from an early date, for there was a ward devoted to women only. There is some evidence that in Hospitaller commanderies both on the continent and in England there were occasionally sisters as well as the brothers; it is suggested that they may have been laundresses or nurses, but by the end of the 12th century the women were being grouped into convents, where they chiefly devoted themselves to prayer as in 'normal' convents. One such convent was founded in Buckland, Somerset (that is Buckland Minchin, sometimes called *Sororum* [of the Sisters] in acknowledgement of the Sisters of St John). There, 50 sisters wore the habit of St John—the only such convent in England.

Associate Brothers (*Confratres*) and the 'Frary'

Many laymen wished to be associated with the Order, but not to undergo the hardships and dangers involved in full membership. This type of membership was in being at least as early as 1111, and increased greatly in the succeeding years. Besides enjoying the good feeling of furthering the Crusades, they shared the spiritual benefits of the order, and were allowed burial in Hospitaller cemeteries.[12] A possible candidate would approach the commander of the local Hospitaller house, and a Chapter would be assembled. He would swear on the Gospels to defend the Order and its possessions, and promise that each year he would present a gift to the Order, generally on the feast of St John the Baptist (24 June). The commander would formally receive him with the Kiss of Peace, and his name and promised donation would be inscribed in a book, though the donation was not compulsory. (The lay associates lived on their own properties, the full Brothers in a Hospitaller house which was generally referred to as the 'convent'.)[13]

The associate Brothers' promise of an annual gift gave rise to the annual Hospitaller collection in aid of the Order, which took place all over the country. Lay clerks on an annual stipend, sometimes one mark, sometimes a pound, were employed to make the collection which was called the 'confrary' or 'frary' (from *confratres*). Each collector was allowed a 'hackney', a stout riding horse, for their work entailed much travelling. The collection took place in local churches, and an address would be given in praise of the Order and the work of the Crusades. It is understandable that the collections were unpopular with the local clergy as can be seen from successive papal bulls ordering the bishops to excommunicate any who used violence against the collectors. Complaints were made that the local clergy were hindering the preaching, and claiming part of the collections. In 1217, 1221 and 1244, successive popes complained that the clergy were not allowing the collectors to make their annual visits, and were molesting them.

Nevertheless it is clear that the frary made a very useful addition to the funds of the Order. In the 1338 Survey this collection is duly listed in the accounts of the various houses; often the entries have a defensive tone: the frary used to be worth so much but now much less. However in no instance is the diminution attributed to the acts of the clergy, but chiefly to the king's imposts:

> *Ansty (Wilts)*: the frary when in good order was worth £40 p.a., but now scarcely £30, and doubtful if so much in future
>
> *Godsfield (Hants)*: the frary used to be 60 marks, now, because of the poverty of the land, taxations of 1/10th and 1/16th of movable goods, the levy of wool, ward of the sea etc., now scarcely 40 marks
>
> *Grenham (Berks)*: Frary used to be worth 27 marks [£17 14s.], sometimes more, sometimes less, and now on account of the poverty of the realm and divers taxes for the king for the defence of the sea, and wool seized throughout the kingdom, scarcely raised £10

Trebyghen (Cornwall): frary used to be 32 marks, now scarce 28

Chibburn (Northumberland): the frary 12½ marks, and no more because it is on the borders of Scotland (because of the Scottish war i.e.) and the rents of assize could scarcely be collected.[14]

Several other entries give the frary as uncertain. The taxation on movable goods was indefensible, for these were lay subsidies from which the Hospitallers as a religious body should have been exempt. The seizing of the wool was equally high-handed. But there can be little doubt that waning enthusiasm for the Crusades must have played its part in the shrinking of the frary, especially towards the end of the crusaders' occupation of the Holy Land.

Hospitality and 'Sweeteners'

Probably echoing the Hospitallers' original ideal of succouring pilgrims to the Holy Land, most of their houses elsewhere (except the smallest, the *camere*), were bound by their Rule and by the conditions of many of their donation-charters, to offer hospitality to passing travellers. It can be seen from the 1338 Survey that it could be a costly item in the budget of a local house. Food and drink were provided for travellers and fodder for their horses. Often the actual cost is concealed in the general expenses of the house, as, for example, at Dalby (Leicester):

Expenses of the preceptor, his fellow Hospitaller, the Chaplain and others of the household, and of others visiting, in the name of hospitality—wheat, £8 8s, ale, £10 8s, fish, meat £13, oats for the horses of the preceptor and the visitors—£8.

At Quenington (Gloucester) the expenses of the house are listed for the preceptor, two brother knights, two clerks of the confrary, the rest of the household, and visitors (in the name of hospitality as decreed by the founders of this house).

At Slebech (Pembroke) the sum of £15 was expended on bread for the household, which is admittedly rather a large one as it includes four pensioners (*corrodaries*) as well as three Brothers, a chaplain, an esquire, a chamberlain, a dispenser and the usual list of estate workers, but it concludes this item with the addition of many visitors from Wales who flood in day after day and are great devourers (*devastatores*) without number. Wales also provided a great many (*quamplurimum*) visitors to the house at St Wolstan (unidentified, a member of Garway, listed under Monmouth).

But it is clear that Clerkenwell (the London headquarters of the Order in England) bore the heaviest burden of hospitality. Wheat for bread ran to 430 quarters a year, costing over £170, and malt for the ale 413 quarters, at over £82. This was to feed the normal staff and servants and almost twenty pensioners (*corrodaries*) plus visitors. Kitchen expenses which normally included fish and meat, amounted to over £121. These are heavy sums in medieval money, and the accountant notes at the end that there were innumerable expenses incurred in the name of hospitality, for members

4 17th-century concept of a Hospitaller, engraved by Wenceslaus Hollar, from W. Dugdale's *Monasticon Anglicanum, The Epitome* (1693). Note Clerkenwell in the background.

5 The Priory of the Hospital of St John, Clerkenwell, from an engraving by Wenceslaus Hollar, 1656, illustrated in Sir E. King, *The Knights of St John …* (1934).

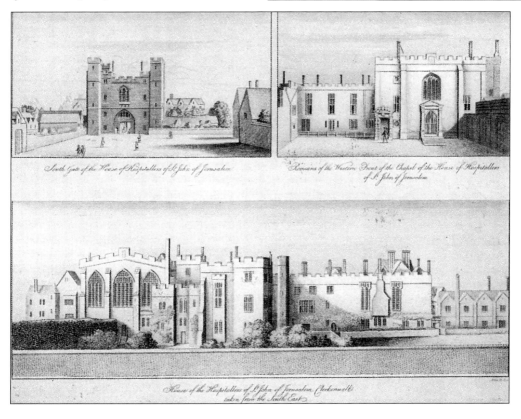

South Gate of the House of Hospitallers of St John of Jerusalem

Remains of the Western Front of the Chapel of the House of Hospitallers of St John of Jerusalem

House of the Hospitallers of St John of Jerusalem, Clerkenwell taken from the South East

of the king's household, and the households of other magnates of the realm, besides preceptors, Brothers and their retinue, coming to conduct business in the king's courts, or other business in the city of London, continuously staying at Clerkenwell until their business was concluded. Perhaps the Prior (head of the Order) and the Procurator General needed the gallon of best ale which they took to their rooms at night.[15]

Clerkenwell's income in 1338 had amounted to £400 (of which £111 had come from ex-Templar rents allocated to the upkeep of the headquarters). Expenditure was over £421; thus, it was the only Hospitaller establishment that year which had failed to provide a surplus for the Treasury, to support the burdens of the Order. Thirty-five other houses, with eight of the smaller establishments (the *camere*) had all produced greater or less surpluses; as many as 20 *camere* were let out, presumably because the Hospitallers had not the manpower either to fill or to supervise them.[16] In the accounts of some of the houses is the record of payments to local magnates. As the accounts were submitted to the central treasury, and the purpose of the payments is openly acknowledged at least once, it is clear that they reflect official policy from 'on high'.

At Halston (Shropshire, three miles north-east of Oswestry) the accountant notes the outlay of gifts to divers lords and their stewards and secretaries for the liberty of having and maintaining the hospital (there) and for having their help, favour and friendship (100 shillings). At Maltby (Lincs) the 'foreign' expenses of the preceptor are accounted for in his promoting the business of his house, and the gifts to the clerks and bailiffs of the sheriff, and to ministers of the king and other lords (40s). Skirbeck (Holland, Lincs) similarly accounts for the outlay of 40s. Slebech (Pembroke) expended no less than £4 on the 'foreign' business of the preceptor, coming and going supervising his bailiwick and in gifts to the ministers of the lord king and other lords. It is clear that the operation of what in modern (somewhat inelegant) terms is called a 'slush fund' could make a significant impact on the local budgets.[17]

Undoubtedly the ready hospitality, and the operation of the 'slush fund', though making severe inroads into the Order's revenue, must have made the Hospitallers more popular than the more

6 Portrait medal of Sir John Kendal as Turcopolier (the commander of native horse-bowmen, an office held by an English knight), 1480. He was later Grand Prior of England. (From Sir Edwin King, *The Knights of St John ...* (1934), facing p.87.)

austere and aloof Templars. The existence of associate brothers (the *confratres*) also made the Order seem more accessible to the general public, though the collection of the frary often caused friction with the clergy, and perhaps sometimes reluctance to pay amongst the *confratres*. But both Orders were persistently accused of pride and arrogance. A Flemish poet, writing in 1289, depicted a scene based on the satires of Reynard the Fox. Reynard features as the essence of all evils in society; he corrupts the clergy, and the Templars and Hospitallers are imagined as competing for his favours; the Templars' spokesman is unskilled in oratory, relying on naive repetitions of his argument whereas the Hospitallers' is intelligent, marshalling his arguments adroitly. Dr. Nicholson has pointed out that this is consistent with the Templars' inability to defend themselves at their trial. Reynard is unable to choose between the two Orders.[18]

None of the foregoing is to be taken as implying that the Hospitallers were better, or worse, as landlords or lords of manors towards their tenants, in comparison with the Templars. Indeed, when the Peasants' Revolt erupted in 1381, the anger of the servile tenants was directed as savagely against Clerkenwell as against any other lords.[19] (Nor is it to be thought that their more relaxed attitude meant that they fell behind the Templars on the field of battle.)

Chapter 1

New Masters for Balsall

It was in 1312 that the Pope abolished the Templars. He decreed that their properties should pass to another crusading Order, the Knights of the Hospital of St John of Jerusalem, commonly known as the Hospitallers. But a full 10 years were to elapse before the Hospitallers got their hands on Balsall. The king, Edward II, who had lawfully taken the Templars' possessions into his hands when they were arrested, clung on to them for another two years after the Templars' abolition until 1314, systematically asset-stripping them in aid of his starved exchequer. He was followed at Balsall by John Mowbray, heir of Roger Mowbray, the original 12th-century donor of the estate; this flouting of the Pope's decree occurred on many estates, where heirs with some justification considered that they had the right to possession.

John Mowbray followed the king's example, felling timber regardless, until 1322 when he was hanged as a traitor for his support of the Earl of Lancaster, the king's enemy, who was also executed.[1] It was now the Hospitallers' opportunity, though even now there were widespread problems, as is clear from the writ issued to the sheriffs of Lincolnshire and Warwickshire instructing them to go to the manors belonging to St John's and seize all malefactors wasting the Prior's goods and chattels; the manors included Balsall and Fletchamstead.[2]

The new masters near-bankrupt
But a mere six years later in spite of the accession of the ex-Templars' properties the Knights of St John were perilously close to bankruptcy, all their goods and chattels on the point of being seized for debt. Two letters survive from this period, the first to Elyan de Villeneuve, the Master or head of the whole Order, from Thomas Larcher, Prior of England, and many high-ranking officers of the Order; it was dated 20 July 1328, and its purpose was to ask permission for Leonard de Tibertis, prior of Venice, to be installed as Prior in place of Larcher. The reasons for this request are given at some length.

The Order in England was then so heavily in debt that movable goods from the houses were being sold off at less than half a fair price, just before the arrival of

7 Carpenters constructing a timber-framed building (1531). From L.F. Salzman, *Building in England down to 1540* (O.U.P., 1952). (Reproduced by permission of Oxford University Press.)

Leonard de Tibertis whom the Master had sent as his deputy to try to rescue the Order from ruin and to reform the conduct (*mores*) of the Brothers. An account of his financial activities is given; briefly, by dint of paying off £185 from income and £4,555 from borrowed money he managed to fend off the Bardi, bankers of Florence, and the merchants of Perugia, the chief creditors. The best terms he could get for the loan was at 25 per cent; this was clearly an emergency measure in a severe crisis, but it gave the Order a breathing space. Leonard had donated his own jewels and had brought others from the Master when he came to England; he had gained the approval of both the King and Queen of England and the gratitude of all the Brothers. The whole Chapter begged that Leonard be made Prior of England.[3]

The second letter was from the King of England to the Pope, asking that he approve the election of Leonard de Tibertis to the Priory of England. The king writes that he sympathises with the plight of the brothers of the Hospital, who,

> though augmented in no small measure by the annexing of the lands which were once the Templars', nevertheless are oppressed by so great destitution and burdened with such heavy debts that we feared for their complete break-up because of the number of creditors who were trying to snatch away all the movable goods of the Hospital for their debts.

He asks that the Pope allow the resignation of Thomas Larcher, and allow Brother Leonard de Tibertis, Prior of Venice 'whom we know to be a man of great wisdom and industry' to be in charge of the Order instead. He describes Larcher 'as decrepit with old age, and so heavily overweight that he cannot rule himself' much less deal with Hospital business as he should. It was dated March 1329.[4]

At first glance, the acquisition of the Templars' possessions should, as the king suggested, have rescued the Hospitallers from disaster, but at least 13 former Templar estates failed to come to the Hospitallers. Edward II had bestowed some as presents on friends or servants; the manor of Temple Guyting, worth 200 marks a year, he gave to his physician, and Strood, Denny and Temple Hurst to the Countess of Pembroke; other lords acquired other manors by fair means or foul.[5] Many that did pass to the Hospital were in a ruinous state, such as Thornton (Northumberland) where all the houses had been uprooted, carried off, and re-erected elsewhere (a process possible with timber-framed buildings).[6] At Godsfield (Hants) 100 acres of timber were reserved for the repair of Templars' houses at Templecombe and Ansty.[7] Many similar instances can be found. In Scotland all the Hospitallers' own possessions were destroyed by the war against the Scots, properties which once returned 200 marks a year.[8] Temple Balsall itself cannot have been flourishing after the depredations of the King and John Mowbray.[9]

Long-term loss from Thomas Larcher's regime can be glimpsed in the 1338 Survey. It is evident that he was an exponent of what is now popularly called 'short-termism'; for example, the account for Greenham (Berks) notes that there was no profit from livestock, which was sold off at the time of Larcher, though normally the 20 cows and 500 sheep the estate could support helped greatly towards the surplus to be sent to the Treasury.[10] Estates at Huntingdon, Harefield and Newington (Middlesex) all were leased out rent-free, doubtless for a heavy down payment.[11] Other reasons for the Hospitallers' financial predicament, arising from the nature and workings of the Order itself, are discussed elsewhere.[12]

Chapter 2

The Survey of 1338

'Extent of the lands and holdings of the Hospital of St John of Jerusalem in England, made by brother Philip de Thame, Prior of the same Hospital in England in 1338'.[1]

Brother Leonard de Tybertis did not live long to enjoy his priorate in England, for he died in 1330, and Brother Philip de Thame was elected in his place and held office until 1358. No doubt with the horrors of Thomas Larcher's 'reign' in mind, he ordered a review of the Order's possessions in England in 1338. This survey is our first view of the Hospitallers in this country. It says something for the financial acumen of de Tybertis and perhaps of Philip de Thame that, a mere 10 years from near disaster, the combined properties of the Hospitallers and the former Templars were able to return well over £3,000 a year to their treasury (though the many pensions and other expenses reduced this to £2,280)—this in spite of the drawbacks referred to in the last chapter.

The survey does not compare favourably with that taken by the Templars in 1185. No tenants' names and holdings are given, and acreages and values tend to be rounded up. It is recorded that at Balsall there was a manor house with a garden worth 20 shillings a year (presumably in produce). A dovecote was worth 10 shillings annually, and 500 acres of arable were valued at sixpence an acre. There were two parcels of meadow, each 60 acres, one valued at three shillings an acre, the second at two. Old fixed rents ('rents of assize') should bring in £44 (66 marks), and the labour dues and other customs of the bondsmen tenants (*nativi*) amounted to 100 shillings a year. The water mill should bring in 60 shillings and stock-breeding the same amount; profit from underwood was reckoned to be £5. The courts, with their fines and amercements were, as often, a source of useful profit—£5 at Balsall; the revenues of Balsall were also bulked up by the income from Sherbourne church which was 'appropriated' to Balsall.

The income from the former Templar estates at Fletchamstead and Chilverscoton was lumped in with Balsall. They are small, cursory accounts; at Fletchamstead there is a messuage worth 5s. a year, pasture worth 50 shillings, stock-breeding 2½ marks (33s. 4d.), underwood 10 shillings, and 360 acres of arable valued at 4d. an acre (£6).

Chilverscoton is treated even more summarily; no messuage or dwelling is listed though in 1309 the manor house there was refurbished to make a room fit for the king, Edward II, to stay the night of 23/24 June, when on his way to meet Piers Gaveston returning from exile in Ireland, and an excavation in 1970 revealed traces of a building with large deposits of 16th-century domestic pottery.[2] All that is given is a carucate (about 120 acres) of arable worth 60 shillings a year, rents and works (of tenants) bringing in £8 7s. 6d., and meadow and pasture worth £4.

The total income from the three estates is shown as £127 2s. 6d. The account of how this was expended is more revealing. At once we learn that there was living at Balsall the preceptor, Henry de Buckston, a serving brother, not a knight. With him were two companions, one, Simon Dyseny, a knight, and John de Sprottelee, another serving brother. The statement of the living expenses helps to flesh out the picture; they are listed for the preceptor, two brothers and others of the household (*aliis de familia*). These include the preceptor's three pages (*garciones*) and a doorkeeper (*janitor*); all wear livery and are allowed half a mark (6s. 8d.) a year for this and for their wages. There is a clerk for the courts and for writing up the accounts; he has 20s. for his robe and his stipend. Also a cellarer (*claviger*), cook, baker and woodward or forester, who all have one mark (13s. 4d.) for their livery and wages.

A steward (*senescallus*), a man versed in the law, was there to preside over the courts, and his greater status is reflected in the annual 40 shillings for his robe and stipend. Two chaplains celebrated mass in the chapel, with 40 shillings each for their stipends; these would be secular or non-Hospitaller priests, and may not have been resident. The stipend of a chaplain celebrating Mass at Fletchamstead for the souls of the founders (five marks or 66s. 8d.) is included in this list of expenses. The bailiff administering Fletchamstead received two marks for his robe and stipend, also included here. A suspicion that Thomas Larcher may have mortgaged the Hospitallers' future by granting generous life pensions (perhaps for heavy down-payments), arises from two annual pensions granted by him, one £5, the other 5 marks, debited to this account, with a further 2 mark pension which had been granted by the Chapter.

Food for the household consisted of wheaten bread (100 quarters of wheat at 3s. a quarter), meat, fish and 'other necessaries for the kitchen' at 5s. a week, and ale (not of the highest quality, made from malt dredge, a mixture of barley and oats, but probably plentiful) costing £10 a year, from 100 quarters of dredge at 2s. a quarter.

Robes and 'other necessaries' for the preceptor and two brothers came to 104 shillings. Other items were wine, candlewax, and oil for use in the chapel, 5s., and repair of buildings 50s., including those of the 'members' (Fletchamstead and Chilverscoton). An annual six-day visit of the Prior (the head of the Order in England) was a heavy impost—£6. The tally of all outgoings came to £74 19s., leaving 78 marks 3s. 6d. (£52 3s. 6d.) to send to the Treasury.[3]

Chapter 3

The Church (1)

The present church of Temple Balsall has been dated approximately to 1290. This is the estimate of L.F. Salzman, the eminent historian and authority on medieval and later architecture.[1] The present writer, however, feels compelled to disagree with this dating for three reasons, as follows:

1. An estate account of 1309-1310 lists the cost of a gutter between the hall, chambers and chapel; these must therefore be contiguous buildings.[2] This would be a physical impossibility with the present buildings as the church is free-standing. Even before the Old Hall lost its eastern bays (now under the cemetery) the nearest distance between hall and church was over twelve feet.[3]

2. The 1290s are a most unlikely time for the Templars to embark on the ambitious project of building a new church of such imposing character. Both the Templars and the Hospitallers were so seriously depleted by the time they were expelled from the Holy Land that the Pope suggested that they should merge into one Order. Moreover records of the Templar properties in England, including Temple Balsall, from 1308 to 1314[4] reveal widespread neglect and decay, clearly the result of long-standing apathy on the part of the Templars; even the New Temple in London, the Templar head-quarters, was not immune to dilapidation.[5]

3. In the north wall to the left of the altar is a small stone ambry (a niche for holding the communion vessels); on its back wall is a damaged carving of the lower part of a serpent. This has been explained by some as evidence of snake worship by the Templars, though the most exaggerated and fantastic charges levelled against the Order at their trial did not include this heresy. A snake entwined on a staff, however, is a well-known symbol of healing, reflecting the medical and nursing functions of the Hospitallers.

When they took over the estates of their old rivals, forgetting the rigours of the Crusades and their own near-brush with bankruptcy in the 1320s, they seem to have entered an enjoyable, euphoric period, as witness the Pope's admonition of 1343.[6] It is possible that in this expansive mood they may have decided to develop Temple Balsall, for the existing hall and chapel could well have been in need of repair, thus placing the date towards the middle of the 14th century and making it a Hospitaller Church. The stone brackets on the west front of the church may have been intended to join on to a new preceptory, which never materialised.

The further history of the church will be discussed below chronologically, in Chapters 8, 12, 21, 22.

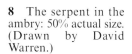

8 The serpent in the ambry: 50% actual size. (Drawn by David Warren.)

Pevsner,[7] like Salzman, viewing the church after the Scott restoration of 1849, declared it all to be late 13th-century in style but assumed that Scott largely rebuilt it. Some of the tracery he finds 'scarcely believable', and asks 'What may she [Lady Anne] have done in her restoration?'. Dugdale[8] described the church as 'in a very ruinous condition' before Lady Anne. In fact there are considerable discrepancies between the description of the windows at the Dissolution,[9] and drawings of the church before the Scott restoration, showing that Pevsner's guess was a shrewd one. Moreover it can be shown that Scott made no drastic alterations except to the bell-turret. In short, the present state of the church is no guide to the date of its original construction.

One item, however, can be attributed to Lady Anne's restoration, beyond argument. A survey of 1910 revealed that the bell in the turret was inscribed: WILLIAM ELDRIDGE MADE MEE 1670. This survey includes a comment (dated 1876): 'William Eldridge of Chertsey was a son of Brian Eldridge who cast several Warwickshire bells in 1651-58 …'.[10]

Chapter 4

The Peasants' Revolt

Between the years 1394 and 1396 events took place in Balsall which brought the manor and its tenants into the national records,[1] conspiracy amongst the tenants, strikes against the labour dues, refusal to pay death duties, and a general defiance of authority. It can hardly be doubted that this episode was inspired by the uprisings of 1381, known as 'The Peasants' Revolt'. These in turn ultimately had their origins in 1349, the year of the plague, the Black Death. This pestilence with its great loss of life had far-reaching effects; one of the chief was the shortage of labour which led to a restive and truculent workforce, and a questioning of the restrictions and obligations of the old order.[2]

Taxation, in the form of poll taxes, finally brought a festering discontent to a head. At the third poll tax in four years the rate was pushed up to three groats (one shilling) on all laymen and women over the age of fifteen. The rough methods of the collectors exacerbated the situation, and by May 1381 the south-east of England was on the verge of revolution. Resistance in several villages in Essex grew into a general rising against the collectors, and houses and manors were sacked, including Cressing Temple, the former Templar manor. Men from Kent and Essex gathered together and chose Wat Tyler, with John Ball, a renegade priest, as their leaders. They marched on London, opening prisons and destroying records when they could lay hands on them, for they hated the manor court rolls which they knew held the details of their servile obligations. They set fire to buildings including the Hospitallers' headquarters at Clerkenwell, which burned for seven days, the rebels not suffering any to quench it.[3]

The mob burst into the Tower of London where the young king, Richard II, was staying, and seized and executed five people including the Archbishop of Canterbury. The king agreed to meet the rebels at Mile End, and there made concessions including amnesty, and abolition of serfdom. Wat Tyler made insolent remarks to the king, was pulled from his horse and killed. This was the end of the rising in London.

But there had been rioting outside London, chiefly against abbeys with the object of burning records, at St Albans, Bury St Edmunds, Ely and in Cambridgeshire the Hospitallers' manor of Duxford, amongst others, was attacked.

9 The burning of the Priory, Clerkenwell, by Wat Tyler. Engraved from Harrison's *History of London*, 1786. (From Sir E. King, *The Knights of St John in the British Empire* (1934), facing p.58.)

When things had settled down, Parliament met and confirmed the amnesty for all but a few specified rebels; the king had gone back on his original promise of abolishing serfdom, and parliament also confirmed this revocation. Little had in fact been changed for the peasants.

Doubtless word of these uprisings would reach the ears of the Balsall tenants, but it was 13 years before there was any open reaction. When Agnes Hert, an unfree tenant, died leaving an only son, a death duty (obit) was due and this was the cause of the unrest. The custom when an unfree tenant died was that if he left a wife and children or a child, after his debts and funeral expenses had been paid, his goods and chattels were divided by the other tenants into three under the watchful eye of the lord of the manor or his servants. One part was to go to the lord, another to the wife and the third to the children. If he should die leaving only a wife, then the division of the goods was into two, one half to the lord, the other to the wife. If he should leave neither wife nor child, the whole was to go to the lord. In the case of Agnes' death, there were only the lord and the son with a claim, and the Hospitallers accordingly demanded a half. Agnes was by no means destitute when she died, and her neighbours found that she had held a messuage (house with some ground and outbuildings), a virgate of land (some 30-40 acres), three mares, four oxen and two cows, valued together at 100 shillings; she also had linen and woollen clothes, vessels of wood and brass, and other domestic utensils, to the value of 60 shillings. The Hospitallers, through Brother Robert Normanton, probably the preceptor of Balsall, required the tenants to let him have his half, but they refused.

Their names were:

	Fines			Fines	
John Clarke (of Mere)	3s	4d	John Janne (or Jaune)	3s	4d
John Ferrour of Oldych	3s	4d	William Pyper	3s	4d
John Foules the elder	6s	8d	John Rowynton	5s	0d
John Foules the younger	3s	4d	William Skynner	5s	0d
John Godeson			William atte Style	5s	0d
Robert Godeson	3s	4d	William Wardeshale ⎱		
John Hull	5s	0d	Margaret his wife ⎰	3s	4d
Richard in the Hurne of Barston	5s	0d	Adam Whaberley	3s	4d
Roger Waryn	6s	8d			

This group, mainly from Balsall, had also some support from the more outlying settlements of Oldych, Barston and Mere. It is noticeable that there is a woman in the group, Margaret Wardeshale, wife of Gilbert, who is willing to stand up and be counted. This was in March 1394.

They then had to await the law's delays. On 14 November 1394 four Warwickshire justices were given a commission to 'hear and determine' what was to be done about 'the bondmen of the Prior of the Hospital of St John in England at Balshale' who have ' long rebelliously withdrawn their customs and services due to him, and are leagued together to resist him besides doing other intolerable evils daily'. What the intolerable evils were is not specified, nor is it clear how long their resistance had lasted. At last on 10 December the same year, the justices met at Coventry, and the offending tenants appeared singly before them sitting with a jury. They could not deny the custom of the obit or their rebellious resistance. They threw themselves 'upon the king's grace', begging to be allowed to settle matters by paying fines, but in accordance with the statute concerning rebellious villeins, they were put in prison.[4] (Conspiracy then, as even now, was viewed very gravely by the law.) Fines were imposed on all of them except John Godeson (and Margaret Wardeshale was joined in a fine of 3s. 4d. with her husband Gilbert). From the scale of the fines John Foules the elder and Roger Waryn, both 6s. 8d., were regarded as the ring-leaders, with John Hull, John Rowynton, William Skynner, and William atte Style next in culpability at 5s. All the rest were fined 3s. 4d. It is not clear how long they were in prison, nor even where, but 'with the assent of the Prior all were liberated from prison'. Two of these names, Wardeshale and Janne (?Jaune) occur in the Templar survey of Balsall in 1185. The name Skinner was current in Balsall in November 1992.

The record of the above events at Balsall and Coventry was rehearsed again in December 1396 when Walter Grendon,[5] the new Prior of St John (the national head, that is), requested information about them, and the happenings already described were detailed for his benefit.[6] Doubtless as the new head of the Order he would wish to be fully informed of such a potentially dangerous situation.

Chapter 5

A Quiet Life Now
Balsall in the Court Rolls, 1412-1415

Even a brief dip into the surviving court rolls for Balsall affords a glimpse into the daily life of the inhabitants.[1] These accounts of the workings of justice at the lowest stage record the misdemeanours, offences, crimes of the population, first as they affect the king's peace (the 'View of Frankpledge' or 'Court Leet'), then the orderly running of the manor for the benefit of its lords (the 'Court Baron', 'manor court' or 'little court'). Offences may range from blocking footpaths to burglary, bloodshed and murder. But no dramatic happenings now disturbed the even tenor of life at Balsall—one shedding of blood only occurs in the first three years of the rolls. There are the usual vexations of life in the country; John of the Field (del Felde) has blocked up Gilmynes Lane with a fence across it. He is to remove this and put in a gate, so that tenants and neighbours can pass. John Ferrour's ditches at Oldych are stopped up; he is ordered to clear them. Reginald Haukserd (a stormy petrel this, who features largely in the rolls) complains that John Ruse took his timber and fuel in Balsall Wood, value 10 shillings. John, first by his attorney, John Gervys,[2] denies this, case postponed till the next court, when Ruse comes 'three-handed' (with three to vouch for him), and 'made his law'; Reginald therefore 'in mercy' (at the mercy of the court); he got off lightly with a threepence fine.[3]

Thomas Bloxwych has a complaint that will strike a chord in many a modern breast; he avers that John Bonde agreed to build a house for him on day-work, but sometimes came to work at the first hour, sometimes at the sixth, to the hurt of Thomas valued at 40d. William Hobben on the other hand complains that Reginald Haukserd and Agnes his wife owe him 12d. as they unjustly detained a pair of hose worth 12d.

Women appear a number of times operating as responsible persons at law. Agnes Baker, widow of John, was administratrix of his goods and chattels, and was accused by Richard Gybon of owing him eight shillings which he says he gave John at Balsall. She has to answer him at the next court. She later complains that Gybon destroyed her grass (herbage) at Bakersplace and Bryghtes with his beasts. A day was given to him to answer. There is a hint of a revenge motive in this exchange. Another widow, Felicia James, executrix of the will of John Hull was similarly accused of not paying her husband's debt, a serious amount of £18.

It is particularly the widows who show up in the rolls, facing up to responsibility on their husband's death. Margaret, the widow of John Wylde, wishing to keep on with the holding, paid 13s. 4d. entry fine to be admitted to a messuage and one virgate of land in Barston, whilst Margaret his daughter claimed a cottage with adjacent croft in Oldych, which Henry Whitewell was occupying; her father had held these by copyhold (the tenure in these cases is recorded on the court roll, and a copy gives a good title). After the death of her father it should have come to Margaret. A prolonged law suit follows.

Doubtless the memory of events of 1394, less than twenty years before, was still fresh in the minds of the Balsall tenants when obits fell due in 1412. The widows resorted to a form of tax evasion still well-known, and legal, today. Roger of the Stable (del Stable) had died and when the obit was claimed Alice his widow had no goods because *in her lifetime* she gave them all to her son William to keep, so he said. (There is a flavour of disbelief in the last three words, which are used by accountants in these kind of claims, probably as a device to save themselves from criticism.) William came to court and claimed the holding as son and heir of Roger and Alice and was admitted to the holding. He did fealty, that is, swore to be true to the lords of the manor, and was told to bring the copy of the roll to the next court. The phrase 'in her lifetime' seems to be used advisedly; the upshot might have been less favourable if it could be shown that she had only parted with the chattels on the death of her husband, an obvious attempt at evasion.

John Clarke of Mere was one of the rebels in 1394 and was then fined 3s. 4d. He died in the year 1412-13, and his childless widow Annabel was due to pay the obit, but had no goods or chattels. John was a tithing-man and a juror—a little above the average, one might think, but there is no suggestion of evasive 'gifts', though in this case the Hospitallers would have been entitled to a half. It could be that after debts were paid there was nothing left, of course; Annabel claimed to hold her husband's tenement and was told to be at the next court to do fealty to the lords.

It is hard to say whether in the cases of Alice and Annabel the Hospitallers (also with 1394, and indeed 1381 in mind) were showing a touch of leniency. But when John Waryn died an obit of 6s. 8d. was due from his widow Juliana, and presumably paid, for she claims his holding and is told to be at the next court to do fealty. Roger Waryn was one of the two chief ring-leaders in 1394, and the likely family connection between him and John may have influenced this impost.

There is no suggestion that, once the rebels had been quelled, they continued to withhold their services from the lords—they knew what to expect.

In these rolls occupations are rarely touched upon, but John Broke, carter, complained that William Hobben (presumably a wheelwright) had promised to repair his cart, to replace a felloe and strengthen the wheels with nails but had broken his agreement. William Mille, miller, was unpopular because he raised the water in the millpond above its normal limits and so flooded his neighbour's meadow and also the highway. One Ball, who is referred to by surname only, often appears for the tenants as their surety, pledged to ensure that they will turn up in court to answer when required; that this was no mere formality is clear when he was fined for the non-appearance of John Ruse to answer Reginald Haukswerd in a plea of debt. Ball is evidently a clerk or a person of some standing and trustworthiness.

It is too late for surnames to be taken literally as indicators of occupation, but the name of William Nelder suggests a needle-making ancestor, and Needlers End is still the name of an area of Balsall, now called Balsall Common. (A more positive indication of needle-making occurs in a record of 1354, when William de Hasele of Balsall was arrested at Balsall for stealing 10 oxen and three cows from Gilbert le Nedlere.)[4] Gurdeler's End is similarly suggestive. A rare piece of information is the description of John Lydyate as weaver; he seems to be a cut above the average for he and his wife took a lease from the Hospitallers on a messuage in Barston for 100 years. Thomas Wever of Coventry has some kind of holding in Balsall, and should have attended the courts but defaulted. Again the name is to be treated with caution, but there seem to be hints of connections with trades and occupations of Coventry, where girdle-makers and weavers are common from the 14th century onwards. One name calls for comment—Richard Leper; Robert le Lepere occurs in Balsall in the Survey of 1185, and the use of 'le' suggests that he may well have been a sufferer, perhaps as a legacy from the Crusades. It is interesting to see a descendant still in the same locality.

The activities of this small community emerge from the rolls and demonstrate the system devised to ensure its peaceable and orderly running. The 'View of Frankpledge' was a six-monthly *review*; the frankpledge was the body of the inhabitants, divided into tithings (10 families) all mutually responsible as 'pledges' for each other's good behaviour. A member of the tithing was elected as tithing-man (somewhat similar to a petty constable), and he would 'present' offenders at the courts. Boys from 12 years old should be in a tithing, and Thomas Castell came to court voluntarily and put himself in a tithing, but John Godson junior, Richard Nevet and John Walshmon, all twelve or more, were presented as not in a tithing and were fined one penny each. They evidently could not produce the fines, and it was ordered that they be distrained against the next View. John Walshmon had been resident for a year and a day, and was perhaps an incomer who after that lapse of time was obliged to join a tithing.

The brewing of ale for sale strictly needed a licence, a regulation almost universally ignored by the local housewives. But 'ale-tasters' were appointed at the Court

Leet (View of Frankpledge) to overlook the quality of ale on offer and note the brewings; a fine of twopence a time for these was so routine at the view that it was virtually the equivalent of a licence. In most villages a handful of housewives might turn an honest copper by selling ale to neighbours or passers-by, and they would advertise a brew by tying a bush to a pole outside the house.

10 Alewife making a sale to a traveller. The 'bush' advertises a brew. From J.J. Jusserand, *English Wayfaring Life in the Middle Ages …*, translated by L. Toulmin Smith (1909), 132.

Two ale-tasters for Balsall, John Lydyate and Henry Bradnok, presented several inhabitants at the 'assize of ale' for 1412-13. Three names occurred at both the spring and autumn Views—Agnes Castle (two and three brewings), Margaret Jaimes (one and two) and Joan Cok or Cokes (two and three). Alice Skynner and Joan Chamber each had one brewing in spring. All were fined at the rate of twopence a brew. William Bechamp, the only man, brewed in autumn and escaped with a penny fine. Joan Cokes was in further trouble (an extra twopence) because she had not sent for the ale-tasters. Evidently it was up to the brewers to give notice.

Three women from Barston were also involved in the assize of ale. Inhabitants of Barston had to attend the courts at Balsall, for the hamlet, once half Templar, half Hospitaller, now belonged wholly to the Hospitallers. The women were Agnes Judder (brewed once) and Anna Fisher (brewed twice). But Agnes was also fined one penny, along with Agnes Page, for being *regraters* of ale. To regrate was to buy from another seller and resell in the same market or within four miles. As each seller wanted a profit it was naturally objected to as an inflationary process. (This restriction applied to any food stuff.) The two Agneses evidently ran out of their own brew to sell and bought up ale from their neighbours for resale.

An ancient but still-observed custom was invoked by Alice Sherman when she raised the 'hue and cry' against some injury or damage inflicted by Gilbert Pyper. If a felony, such as wounding or robbery, took place on a highway, the victim could shout for help and neighbours hearing the cries were obliged to come and help chase the miscreant. The chase, theoretically, might go on through manors and parishes until the sea was reached! Since Pyper was fined only twopence, it cannot have been too serious an offence. But we note that the only instance of bloodshed during the three-year period involved Gilbert Pyper shedding the blood of John Boteler. A second hue and cry was that of Adam Whaberky against Reginald Haukswerd whose name is increasingly familiar. But again the fine was only twopence.

A further twopence was levied on Joan Clerk for keeping a dung heap on the highway to the nuisance of her neighbours.

Tenants from two other hamlets (besides Barston which has already been mentioned) attended the Balsall View of Frankpledge, namely Fletchamstead near Coventry (an ex-Templar manor) and Chadwick, presumably what is now called Chadwick End. It is surprising to find the latter separately listed as it would seem to be simply a component of Balsall. In the first roll the presentments are negligible; for Fletchamstead Henry Robard the tithing man presented three men, Wm Campion, Thomas Hamslape and Nicholas Bailey for not attending the View, as they ought, and each was fined twopence. The distance from Balsall was no doubt a deterrent. For Chadwick, Geoffrey Orchard the aletaster presented nothing because there had been no brewing there. Six tithing men, William atte Style, Wm Gybbon of Erescote (now Eastcote), John Judder, Richard Asteley, John Bradnock junior and Simon Sharp, reported nothing from Barston except for two ditches stopped up, one in Temple Riding and one in Eastcote Wood. The aletasters' report has already been mentioned. In the second roll, Henry Robard's report for Fletchamstead is illegible, but very short, and the aletaster for Chadwick presented one woman (Isabell) for brewing. The tithing men for Barston, the same team, except that Richard Ruydon takes the place of Richard Asteley, presented three for non-attendance, and Richard Asteley for blocked ditches in Westhill and Worley lanes and for building a wall on the highway. William Yonge is also in ditch trouble at the Newland in Maryot lane and William Mulle is instructed to scour some ditches in Couper Fields. One might speculate that relative distance from Balsall (that is, less under the eye of authority) might account for the lightness of these presentments. The rest of these early rolls are all of 'little courts' only held at times when the View of Frankpledge was not due.

Chapter 6

The 15th and 16th Centuries

Little is recorded of the 15th century apart from the court rolls, but the names of two preceptors are noteworthy, for both attained eminence, and one was executed for treason. Robert Mallory was preceptor of Balsall and Grafton, and it is clear that the two preceptories were now run jointly. He became head of the Order of St John, now called Grand Prior, in 1433. Another Brother, John Langstrother, followed the same route—preceptor of Balsall and Grafton and then Grand Prior in 1470. He had been made Lord Treasurer of England in 1469 and took the side of Lancaster in the civil wars (Yorkists against Lancastrians); he was taken prisoner at the battle of Tewkesbury, which sealed the fate of the house of Lancaster. With other prisoners he was court-martialled, and executed at Tewkesbury in 1471.[1]

11 The execution of the Grand Prior John Langstrother in 1471. (From Sir Edwin King, *The Knights of St John …* (1934), facing p.72.)

Coming to Blows over Balsall

Towards the end of the 15th century the Hospitallers were no longer dwelling at Balsall. Whether it was that by then they no longer had the manpower to cover all the preceptories (or commanderies as they now began to be called), or whether, as has been surmised, they preferred to live at Grafton, cannot now be proved.[2] At any rate, by the time of Edward IV (1461-83), John Beaufitz, Esquire, had the lease of the Old Hall (and probably the whole manor), and was living there. He was the Escheator (investigator of lands forfeit to the Crown) for Warwickshire and

Leicestershire, and Justice of the Peace for Warwickshire at one time or another.[3]

In 1496 John Kendal, Grand Prior of the Order of St John in England, leased the commandery of Balsall to Robert (later Sir Robert) Throckmorton for three years at £184 13s. 4d. a year, with the proviso that he 'keep due and convenient hospitalitie and one honest and able prest to minyster divine service in the said commandery'. The lease was to be renewed every three years, up to twenty years. But before Robert could enter Balsall, one Robert Bellingham, described as 'the king's serjeant porter', had to be evicted (he had been ordered to leave, and refused).[4] Sir Robert then held the estate until Prior Kendal's death in 1503. His successor as Grand Prior was Sir Thomas Dokwra, a man of European reputation and by far the most prominent figure in the Order at that time (in 1521 he was the prime candidate for the vacant post of Grand Master of the whole Order). He

12 Portrait of Sir Thomas Dokwra, Grand Prior of England, 1503-1527. (From Sir Edwin King, *The Knights of St John ...* (1934), facing p.92.)

refused to renew Sir Robert's lease, but allowed him to hold the commandery for one more year on condition that he paid up the arrears of rent (over £150), and that if Sir Launcelot Dokwra came home from Rhodes and wanted to occupy Balsall, Sir Robert would leave the place vacant for him. Sir Launcelot was almost certainly a kinsman of Sir Thomas. (It appears that when the Hospitallers had served abroad for some time, they were awarded their '*chevisse*' or '*chevissement*', that is, a commandery in England when it fell vacant, where they were to live.)

Sir Launcelot duly came from Rhodes, probably in 1524 after the surrender of the island to the Turks. He was accompanied by a fellow-knight, Sir Thomas Sheffield, and 'certain justices of the peace' (evidently expecting trouble). They approached Balsall with the object of taking over the commandery, but Sir Robert Throckmorton with his brother Richard had fortified the manor house (the Old Hall) and refused them admission.[5] It was alleged that Sir Robert had unofficially sub-let it to Richard.

Sir Robert and his brother were summoned to appear before the council sitting in the Star Chamber. To guard Balsall during his absence Sir Robert installed one Arthur Wylcokkes, chaplain, and other persons, who sold the hay and 'did other waste and injury'. The situation was clearly not resolved, for further actions took place in 1528-30.[6]

In 1528, one Martin Dockwra, a kinsman of Thomas Dockwra, appeared as plaintiff in the court of the Star Chamber against Sir George Throckmorton, son of Sir Robert (who died in 1518) and sheriff of the counties of Warwick and Leicester in 1526-27. The issue was the forcible dispute as to the manor of Balsall'.[7]

Sir George deposed that Thomas Dockwra had leased Balsall to Martin Dockwra for an unspecified term of years, with the proviso that if the Prior, being also commander of Balsall, wished to dwell there, Martin should leave and give place to him. On the death of Thomas Dockwra in 1527, William Weston was elected Prior of the Order and also commander of Balsall. He now wished to keep Balsall in his own hands 'for his own commoditie and pleasure', so on 20 May 1328 he gave Martin notice to quit in a year's time. Martin accepted the notice and wrote that he had got a little house nearby for himself and his wife. When the year was up the Prior sent one Richard Hawks and other servants to take possession in his own name and for his own use. Hawks entered peaceably, then held a court in the Prior's name, when he asked for the fealty of Martin for land which he had bought in Balsall and also the fealty of the other tenants, both free and copyhold. All swore to be true tenants of the Prior, but when Hawks asked Martin to take his goods and household out of the manor house (the Old Hall), he refused. Disputes arose, and the Lord Chancellor (Cardinal Wolsey) fearing serious unrest sent writs to both the Prior and Martin Dockwra to quit until the issue was settled, and another to Sir George Throckmorton asking him to take possession until the king's pleasure be known.

The Prior obeyed the writ, but Martin gathered into the dwelling house various persons from Knowle Sanctuary (Knowle church was less than two miles away)— thieves and murderers 'and other Riotous and ill-disposed persons', 15 and more of them—to keep the house forcibly. Sir George approached, but dared not enter for fear of his life, so he departed, leaving some of his servants to prevent the sanctuary men from escaping back to Knowle, but, with the help of Martin Dockwra's chaplain, three of the ringleaders got out during the night, and armed with bows and arrows made their way back to the Sanctuary.[8]

The next day Sir George deposed that on 7 October 1529 with some of his servants and some tenants of Balsall, as many as thirty, he came to Balsall and entered the hall *peaceably*, but some of the thieves were in a chamber with the wife of Dockwra with the door locked. Sir George broke open the door and arrested two thieves, John Edwardes and William Somer, and sent them to Warwick goal; he caused the wife and other unauthorised persons to leave, and at last took possession of the Old Hall.[9]

Dockwra's version of this last incident was that Sir George came with up to 30 supporters (13 named) 'in a riotous and warlike manner and with great force and

13 Knowle Church.

violence' entered the house, 'broke open the chamber door' and 'haled out' Isabel, the wife of Dockwra, shouting 'kill her!', 'slay her!' until she was in fear of her life.

Claims and counterclaims, answers, replications, rejoinders and reminders succeeded each other, leaving voluminous records of the Star Chamber proceedings. Lesser characters in the drama deposed in their turn. At one juncture the Constable of Balsall gave his evidence. This was Henry Paynter of Balsall, husbandman, sent for to keep the king's peace. He called on the occupants of the Old Hall to come out, but they kept the doors fast. Three supporters of the Constable, Edward Turkey, Robert Fyssher and John Sidnall, then lunged at the door with a pole, and the Constable put his bill between the door and the post and broke open the lock. They expelled one John Wynne. Asked about the threat to Isabel, the Constable said that one man had said those words, but he could not remember who it was. He mentioned incidentally that they found over 15 score of cheeses in the house. On another occasion when he was there with Throckmorton servants they took out of the house two barrels of butter and other victuals.[10]

Chapter 7

Isabel the Survivor

The outcome of the disturbances related in the last chapter is a surprising one, for as late as 1552, Isabel the widow of Martin Docwra (by then married to one Giles Foster) was the sitting tenant at Balsall. Evidently she was a survivor *par excellence*, for there she was with her new husband, back in the Old Hall from which she had so ignominiously been ejected over twenty years before. The death of her first husband and Henry VIII's dissolution of the Hospitallers in 1540 seem to have passed her by.[1]

William Weston and the Old Hall
What had happened to the express wish of the Grand Prior to have Balsall manor house and park for his own pleasure? There was some refurbishment of the Old Hall in the 16th century; the substantial chimney on the outside of the west end is of that date, and it can be shown that the wooden heraldic 'shields' which now adorn the walls of the parlour and chamber above it must predate 1540.

Seventeen shields survive, with five different devices: four with the simple cross of the Order of St John, which should be 'gules a cross argent', but are painted with a cross 'or' (gold); four more are the full arms of William Weston (with the 'cross in chief' used by the Hospitallers of the 'English Tongue'); three are Saracens' heads, and three more are anchors, both crests referring to his active service. The last, unidentified, shield displays an anchor and a tun (barrel); superimposed on the anchor are the letters LIKES. Probably in the restoration of the shields in 1851, the first two letters of ILKESTON were misinterpreted as 'LI'. The crest is clearly a rebus on the name ILKESTON, which was part of the land owned by the Revell family, donated to the use of the Hospitallers.[2] Dugdale[3] shows an additional device, two running (passant) foxes, which were another crest related to the Weston family. He also shows the Saracens' head, but as a blackamoor. It is likely that the restoration of 1851 was not the first, for there is an affidavit on the back of one of the shields to the effect that the original colours were faithfully followed.

Whatever the case, it is evident that the heraldry relates almost entirely to Weston; a decree in Chancery suggests that the Grand Prior may have had the tenancy of

14   Heraldic shields in the Old Hall.
1. The coat of arms of William Weston (his mother was sister and heiress of John Camel of Shopwick). (4)
2. The Saracen's Head, the crest of William Weston. (3)
3. The Anchor, probably awarded as a crest to William Weston in acknowledgement of his prowess at sea. (3)
4. A reference to the Revell family who owned Ilkeston painted LIKES in error. (3)
5. The Cross of St John. (4)
The number of examples of each heraldic emblem is in brackets.

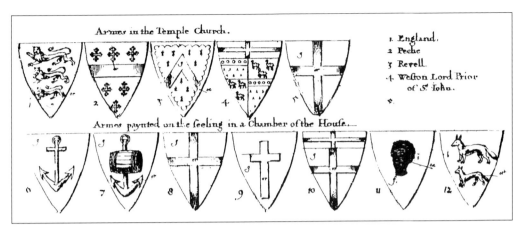

15   Shields at Temple Balsall, illustrations from Wm Dugdale's *Antiquities of Warwickshire* (1730), II, 969. Note the arms said to be in the church at that time: England, Peche, Revell, William Weston, Grand Prior, and the Order of the Hospital of St John. John Peche held the manor of Balsall for a time during the King's pleasure after the execution of John Mowbray (Cal. CL. Rolls, Edward II, 1321-4, no.215 Nov 2, 1322) when it was forfeit to the King because of his treason. Hugh Revell was Grand Master of the Order 1258-1277. For the arms in the Old Hall, see p.30.

Balsall from 1529 to 1535, and there seems little doubt that he was responsible for the refurbishment of the Old Hall and seriously intended occupying it, perhaps on his retirement. Isabel had been pursuing her claim through the courts, and initially lost her case, but on 28 June 1535 a decree in Chancery annulled a former decree 'in the suit of Isabella, widow of Martin Docwra, versus Sir William Weston, Prior of St John of Jerusalem concerning a lease made to Martin by the late Prior, Sir Thomas Docwra, of the commandery of Balsall Warwickshire', and so her persistence paid off.[4]

Brother (Sir) William Weston gave distinguished service to his Order. He commanded the Post of England at the siege of Rhodes, and was wounded in the action in May 1523. After the evacuation of the island he was placed in command of the sailing ships of the Order, and commanded 'the first Ironclad vessel'. He returned to England and became Grand Prior of the Order in 1527.[5]

The Hospitallers refused to deny the supremacy of the Pope at the request of Henry VIII, and the Order was dissolved by Act of Parliament in April 1540. William Weston died on 7 May.

A brief glimpse of life at the Old Hall is afforded by a letter of 1545. It is from Giles Foster, dated at Balsall 'this Trinity Sunday', and addressed to Anthony Bourchier, auditor to Queen Catherine Parr. In recompense for Anthony's kindness to him he is sending a gelding—'no better nag for labour than he'—and venison—'half a buck, as good as my ground bears at this season'.[6] It is interesting to see Foster, merely the husband of the tenant, referring in lordly fashion to the deer park at Balsall as 'my ground', only five years after the Hospitallers' estates were confiscated to the Crown.

Chapter 8

Balsall in 1541
including The Church (2)

In January 1541 Henry VIII's commissioners came round to Balsall to make a survey, to tot up what their master had now got his hands on, with attention to removable materials such as lead, iron or bell-metal which readily convert to cash.

> First the scite of the Temple or Manor of Balsall, with a fair green courte at the entre, containing by estimation 1½ acres, at the east end inclosed, partly with Pale and partly with lodgings; on the south side, with a great Barn with 2 porches, containing 9 Bays, and at the end of the same a Garner of 1 Bay, and a garden and dovehouse, and at the back of great barn a yonge orchard. The west end of the court inclosed with stables and houses for hay under 1 roof, containing 10 bays, tiled. On the north side standing the chapel and a manor place which is at the entre in an olde hall, at the west end of the same a fayre parlour, cealed, with a chimney and glass windows, with fair lodging over the same, and adjoining, a fair Buttery with a cellar under the same, and at the east end of the hall, divers fair lodgings above and beneth a fayre lowe parlour with a chimney, and a great glass window opening upon the said courte, and on the north side of the hall, the kitchen and other houses of office, which is worth by yere with a fayre Chappell to the same place belonging—35s. 8d.[1] [Punctuation supplied]

The Kitchen and 'other houses of Office' have been identified from estate accounts of 1308,[2] and the buttery, or rather the cellar under it, was revealed by an excavation of 1981 (see below pp.84-91). The extension on the east end of the hall, in the shape of the 'fayre lowe parlour', has since disappeared but a map of 1759[3] shows just such an extension, projecting on the south side as well as the east. The gap between this extension and the church is shown as closed by a five-barred gate, which with its posts would span only about 12 feet. But the gap between hall and church is now some 40 feet, leaving a discrepancy of 28 feet which would accommodate two 14-foot bays.

The commissioners noted that the 'fayre parlour' (the ground floor of the west wing of the building) was 'cealed', that is, had a ceiling, and not exposed beams, as now; they mention the chimney and the fact that, exceptionally at that date, the windows were of glass (rather than wooden lattice 'filled up with wicker or fine rifts [slivers] of oak').[4] It is disappointing that they do not itemise the heraldic shields on the ceiling, but these, being so decidedly irrelevant with the dissolution of the Hospitallers, may have been regarded as simply of no monetary value and so not worth recording. (It is unthinkable that any later tenant or lord of the manor would order the construction and erection of these artefacts.)

The western parlour with its chimney was balanced with a 'fayre lowe parlour with a chimney at the east end' (already mentioned) with a 'great glass window' looking out on the courtyard. It is difficult to interpret the phrase 'divers fair lodgings above and beneth' this second parlour, all having since disappeared under the cemetery ground.

The description of the 'fayre Chappell' belonging to the hall is of particular interest.[5] This, of course, was the present church. The chief difference was a roodscreen 'of old painted timber dividing the quire from the body of the church, whereon standeth a rood [crucifix] with divers old images of timber'.

From outside the chapel is described as 35 yards long, with battlements one yard wide (high), the roof 'very full of old timbers, covered with shingle with lead on top'. The steeple is a 'very little one covered with board interlaced with lead', and there were 'two small bells of one accord, with two claps, and one bell broken and cracked, the three weighing 'by estimation CCC di' (3½ hundredweight).

There is a considerable amount of painted glass. The body (nave) of the church is said to contain two great windows of three lights of painted glass, with little iron. The west window has five lights, two 'white' and three painted, again with little iron. The choir has the east window, five lights of painted glass. The text now seems to be suspect, for there are said to be 'two windows of three lights of painted glass, and two windows of three lights on the one side of the choir'. The question of these windows and Lady Anne Holbourne's restoration will be discussed below (Chapter 12).

Turning to the interior we find a holy water stoup lined with lead and a timber font also lined with lead 'with a small barr of iron over'. No smallest piece of metal escapes notice. There were three long forms and 13 little ones, the rood screen already mentioned, and two 'altar stones'. On one side of the choir was a 'frame of desks and thirteen seats of old timber' and a pew 'with certayn old stooles or forms of timber'.

The rest of the inventory of the interior concerns the 'implements ... of the late lord of St Johns', vestments and hangings, and miscellaneous items such as two old tin candlesticks, a little cross of timber 'covered with gilded lead', an old pyx, an old mass book, an old censer, another little cross with staff (presumably a processional cross), an old cruet (the vessel used to hold wine or water for the services), two more old candlesticks 'and a little one of tyne', an offertory box with hanging lid and chain and an iron 'braunche to sett lights on'. The next item appears to be the pulpit—'the scale [stair] and all the frame with images of Our Lady and St John of old timber'.

There was an altar cloth of 'old sarsenet' (a thin silk), a cloth of 'old worne silk, two curtains of old silk'. A vestment of 'old chamlett with a Red Cross' was presumably left by the Templars over two hundred years earlier; another of old damask had red velvet in panels, worn and torn, yet another with cope, alb and tunicle of old silk. Finally, a little bell.

It is noticeable that everything is old, worn out, or damaged.

The commissioners then rounded up a few outstanding items: 'the great lead' (lead brewing vessel) set in a 'furnace', a brick or stone foundation with a fire-grate below to heat the water for brewing; this was in the brewhouse. In the hall was a coffer with 'evidences', that is, evidence to title or title-deeds to parts of the estate; also in the hall was a silver chalice, parcel-gilt, said to be worth about eight shillings and fourpence, 'which Mr Foster saith his predecessor, Mr. Dockwra there did leave'—a reminder of the troubled days of Martin Dockwra and Giles Foster's long and fortunate sojourn at the Temple.

Chapter 9

The Park

The grounds over which Giles Foster lorded it were surveyed, along with the rest of the estate, by Henry VIII's commissioners in 1541:

> Item a goodly parke adioyninge to the house and courte aforesaid, paled about and replenysshed with dere to the number of 100 by estimation, conteyning 277 acres, whereof 2 pooles 2 acres besides sufficient pasture for the said dere ... in the parke 7 score 17 acres of fayre tymber oakes of 100 years growth.[1]

A plan of 1759 shows 10 fields with the word 'park' in their name, and these have been taken as a basis for deducing the site and extent of the park.[2] Park Corner on Temple Lane (also the name of the adjoining close) and Balsall Lodge Farm (from its name) may be regarded as further clues, as also the close called 'The Lawn', for clear spaces among wooded parks were once called *launds*, and it is only in modern times that 'lawn' has come to mean a purely ornamental grassed area. As this is over 28 acres and it appears in this plan over two hundred years ago, its name clearly has the older meaning.

Old Green Lane, Temple Lane and Fen End Road, together with the cart track passing Balsall Lodge Farm and linking Fen End Road with Old Green Lane, seem to form natural boundaries. The park is described as adjoining the house (the Old Hall), and the line of the Bread Walk continuing down over the brook to the present kissing-gate and beyond may be taken as the north-west limit. The area within these bounds is probably the early park of the Templars.

The Templars had a park at Balsall as early as 1195. It was probably never intended as a deer park; indeed the Templars were originally against hunting, and at their dissolution there were neither deer nor venison on the estate, nor does a park-keeper appear amongst the workforce of the manor.[3] The purpose of this early park was to enable the Brothers to exercise themselves and their horses, and to have a measure of privacy. They would also have profited from the timber and coppice, and the pasture which later fed the deer would have provided forage for their horses.

But field-walking reveals a ditch (X-Y on map) some four to five feet deep in places, running from north to south on the west side of this older park, hiving off a sector which includes Lime Tree Park, Park Corner and Park Lays. This, together with the boundaries already mentioned, probably encloses the deer park of the Hospitallers, reducing the older park by a sizable stretch of land on the west.

It contained two pools, Great Pool which once watered the deer, on the line of the X-Y ditch, now filled in and bisected by a hedge-line north of Gravely Park, and the southernmost pool, much silted up and largely taken over by reeds.

16 *(above)* Remains of southern pool.

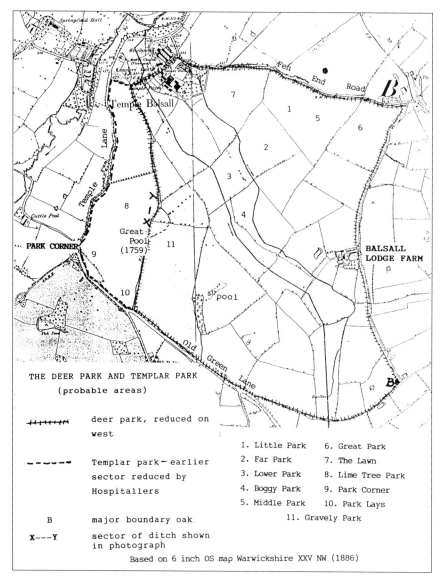

THE DEER PARK AND TEMPLAR PARK
(probable areas)

┿┿┿┿┿┿┿   deer park, reduced on
            west

▬ ▬ ▬ ▬ ▬   Templar park – earlier
            sector reduced by
            Hospitallers

     B   major boundary oak.

X━━━Y   sector of ditch shown
            in photograph

1. Little Park	6. Great Park
2. Far Park	7. The Lawn
3. Lower Park	8. Lime Tree Park
4. Boggy Park	9. Park Corner
5. Middle Park	10. Park Lays
	11. Gravely Park

Based on 6 inch OS map Warwickshire XXV NW (1886)

17 *(left)* The Deer Park, based on Tomlinson's map of Temple Balsall (1759), Warwick CRO CR 621/6 and OS six-inch map, 1886, Warwickshire, sheet XXV.

18 *(below)* Deep ditch running down west side of the park (X–Y on map).

The acreage of the area suggested as the deer park amounts to some 360 acres, as against 277 acres in the 1541 survey. But often in medieval (and later) times a non-standard or 'customary' measure was used locally; in Warwickshire they might write that 'it was measured by the great perch', so that the acres thus measured were some 35 per cent bigger than the modern statutory acre. If this was the case at Balsall, the 277 acres of 1541 should correspond to about 374 modern acres. The total of 360 falls below this, but the discrepancy of 14 acres is not enough to invalidate the general outline suggested in the map. The 1541 figure was probably estimated rather than measured, as was the number of deer. Certainly the acreage of the Great Pool was considerably out at one acre ('2 pooles 2 acres') for on Tomlinson's map it is over three acres (3 0 19).[4]

It is worth noting that the park was 'paled about', which would also keep the

19   Prospect of the park looking north.

20   Park boundary oak, Old Green Lane at B
on map. Girth at 4 ft., over 15½ ft.

deer out of the immediate purlieus of the
house and also of the church and cemetery. The large boundary oak (**B** on map)
is also noteworthy; its girth at four feet is
over 15½ feet.

Chapter 10

Henry VIII, Mary, Elizabeth

In this unsettled period, the lordship of Balsall and its members (or the entitlement to it on reversion) passed from hand to hand, probably with little effect on the daily life of the manor. Henry VIII had married Catherine Parr in 1543 as his sixth wife, and the next year settled some 25 manors on her as her jointure, that is, for her life after his death. They included Temple Balsall and its members, Ryton, Grafton (both originally Hospitaller manors) and Fletchamstead. The reversion of the manors, to fall due after Catherine's death, was granted to Edward Seymour, Duke of Somerset and Lord Protector. (Before his attainder and death for treason he had the Priory church [St John's] at Clerkenwell blown up with gunpowder and used the stones to build Somerset House in the Strand.)[1] After his attainder the manor of Balsall came to John Dudley, Earl of Warwick, and after *his* attainder, to Edward Sutton, Lord Dudley, in 1554.

The accession of Queen Mary put everything into the melting-pot. Her goal was to restore England to the embrace of Rome, and as part of this plan she made moves to re-found the Order of St John, putting Sir Thomas Tresham at its head as Grand Prior and giving him, amongst other assets, the reversion of the manor of Balsall.[2] In 1555 Lord Dudley surrendered the manor to the Crown, and probably the plan was to give the Grand Prior full title. It is interesting to see that in this surrender the manor is called 'Templefarme, county Warwick, and a watermill called "Fourdemylle" in Templefarme', a pointer to the site of the mill (probably at Barston Ford).[3]

With Queen Mary's death in 1558, and Elizabeth's accession, all Mary's plans came to nothing. In 1566 Elizabeth gave Balsall to Robert Dudley, Earl of Leicester, and he granted the reversion of the manor after his own death and that of his wife, to his brother Ambrose, Earl of Warwick for life, with a remainder (possession after the death of Ambrose) to Robert Dudley, the Earl of Leicester's illegitimate son by Lady Douglas Howard, Countess of Sheffield, who was born in 1574.[4]

Balsall and the Dudley family
The manor now began to settle down and move towards its modern and permanent status, its settlement in perpetuity as a charity. But before that there were complications

21   Douglas, Lady Sheffield, who married for her second husband Robert Dudley, Earl of Leicester and had issue by that marriage Sir Robert Dudley Kt known in Florentine history as *il Duca di Nortombria.* (No provenance is given for this portrait.)

stemming initially from the vexed question of Robert Dudley's illegitimacy.

Lady Douglas claimed that there had been a secret marriage between herself and the Earl in 1571, secret from fear of Elizabeth's displeasure at evidence that Robert, her favourite courtier, was not solely devoted to herself. But Lady Douglas was obliged to give up her hopes of the alleged marriage being acknowledged when in 1578 Leicester married Lettice Knollys, daughter of Frances Knollys. The next year Lady Douglas herself married Sir Edward Stafford, leaving her five-year-old son Robert in the care of his father the Earl of Leicester.[5]

Hard on his marriage, in August 1578, Robert Dudley made his will, written in his own hand, probably intending it as part of the marriage settlement.[6] He made his new wife Lettice his sole executrix. He bequeathed a magnificent jewel to Queen Elizabeth, a setting of three great emeralds with diamonds and a rope of 600 pearls to hang it on. He had already settled his wife's jointure before the will, but added many properties to it, and gave instructions to sell others to defray his debts. He did not forget 'my base son', Robert, who at the first drafting of the will in 1578 was only four years old, but all the bequests to him (including Balsall and Long Itchington, land at Wanstead and in Lancashire), were conditional upon the death of one person or another.

The 'base son' had from early years devoted himself to the study of mathematics and everything related to naval affairs, and when he was only 21 was invested by Queen Elizabeth in the command of three ships of war; with these he sailed to Trinidad and attacked and captured some Spanish vessels; in 1596 he joined the Earl of Essex in his expedition against Cadiz and was knighted for his bravery.[7]

He kept quiet until the death of Elizabeth in 1603, when he was 29, and then set about trying to prove that his father and mother were legally married and laying claim to the earldoms of Warwick and Leicester. He failed in this attempt and in high dudgeon left England for good in 1605, repudiating his marriage to Alice Leigh with her four daughters; he sailed for Italy with Elizabeth, daughter of Sir Robert Southwell, a noted beauty, dressed as a page.[8]

22 Sir Robert Dudley.
(No provenance of this
portrait is given.)

He settled in Florence and made a great name for himself for his learning and
ingenuity, designing a new class of warship which he hoped the English navy would
adopt, and many mathematical instruments. He achieved what was probably his greatest
ambition when he was created Duke of Northumberland by Ferdinand II, Emperor
of the Holy Roman Empire in 1620; just before his death in 1649 he published his
book *Dell' Arcano del Mare* on naval architecture and navigation.[9]

Sir Robert became a catholic and, obtaining a dispensation from the Pope, married
Elizabeth Southwell. After his death his children remained with the Duke of Tuscany
'in wealth and honour', retaining the titles of Northumberland and Earls of Warwick
and Leicester.[10]

Chapter 11

Duchess Dudley and her Daughters

Sir Robert Dudley received his recognition in 1620, as has been said, but his abandoned wife Alice had to wait another 24 years before any solace came her way. By then England was labouring under the Civil War. A few days before Charles I raised his standard at Nottingham, he appeared with an armed force outside the walls of Coventry. The Parliamentarian city refused him entry. At this humiliating juncture, Sir Thomas Leigh, a staunch Royalist, welcomed and entertained the king at Stoneleigh, and on 1 July 1643 Charles I created him Baron Leigh of Stoneleigh. Sir Thomas was cousin to Alice (Leigh) Dudley, and it is likely that she shared his sympathies, and may have taken the opportunity to press her claim to some recognition, perhaps to ensure some status for her daughters. At any rate, on 23 May 1644, Charles I, remembering the favour done to Sir Robert by the Emperor, gave to Lady Alice the title of Duchess Dudley for her life. She died in 1689, and as her marriage to Robert is said to have taken place before 1597, she must have been a great age as was her grandmother Alice at her death.[1]

She made many benefactions in her life, contributing large sums to the restoration of the Church of St Giles in the Field, augmented the vicarages of Stoneleigh and many other parishes, and left money for the poor of the parish of St Giles and to set poor boys apprentice. There was a tradition of philanthropy in the family; her grandfather, Sir Thomas Leigh, was a wealthy merchant and Lord Mayor of London in 1558; his widow Alice, a wealthy heiress in her own right, built an almshouse in Stoneleigh for five poor men and five poor women. She lived at Stoneleigh to a very advanced age.[2]

Her eldest daughter, Alicia Douglas (thus Christian-named in compliment to her grandmother, Lady Douglas Sheffield), left £2,000 to her mother on her death-bed at the early age of 24, unmarried. This was to be expended on charitable works.[3] She lived with her mother at Dudley House, St Giles, as did her sisters until they married.

The second daughter, Frances, married Sir Gilbert Kniveton of Bradley, South Derbyshire, but little more seems to be known of her. She probably died fairly young.

Lady Anne, the third daughter was the wife, then widow, of Sir Robert Holbourne, a noted lawyer and solicitor-general to Charles I. The youngest, Lady Katherine, left Dudley House to marry Sir Richard Leveson, Knight of the Bath, of Trentham Hall, Staffordshire. In his patent creating Lady Alice Duchess, Charles I declared that 'casting our princely eye upon the faithful services done unto us by Sir Richard Leveson, Knight of the Bath … and also the great services which Robert Holborne Esquire, hath done to us by his learned pen and otherwise …' (the respective husbands), and considering the honour done to their father by the Emperor, granted these two surviving daughters the rank and precedence of a duke's daughters.[4]

Robert Holbourne was knighted soon after this, but died in 1647. Doubtless it was her late husband's eminence in the law that emboldened Lady Anne to instigate (and finance) the long and costly

23 Alicia the second daughter of Sir Thomas Leigh of Stoneleigh Abbey, Knt & Baronet, wife of Sir Robert Dudley Knt, created Duchess Dudley by King Charles I 20 May 1645. (From the original picture in the Collection of His Grace the Duke of Sutherland at Trentham Hall.)

suit in Chancery wherein the inheritance of Temple Balsall (and Long Itchington) was contested after the death of Sir Robert Dudley in Italy which ended his claim. Lady Anne, with Lady Katherine and Sir Richard Leveson, was vouchee in a recovery which was successful in 1656. Lady Anne had bought out Alicia's share, and on the death of Lady Frances it was agreed that she should have her share as well as some recompense for the heavy costs she had incurred at law.[5]

It was the two younger sisters who were of particular importance to Temple Balsall. Before her death in 1663 Lady Anne repaired the church of Temple Balsall and endowed a ministry, and Lady Katherine founded the Hospital or almshouses and the school (she also founded a school at Trentham).

Chapter 12

Two Sisters' Bequests
Lady Anne and the Church
The Church (3)

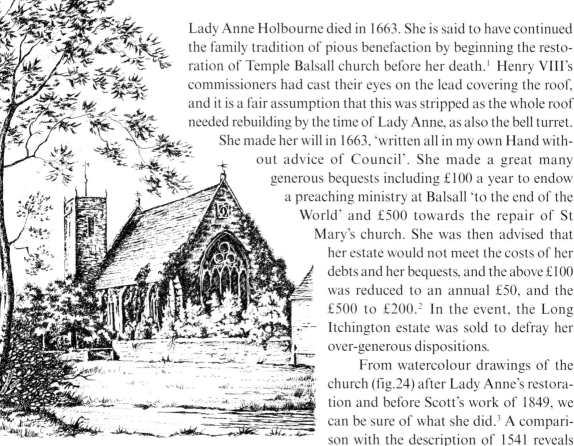

Lady Anne Holbourne died in 1663. She is said to have continued the family tradition of pious benefaction by beginning the restoration of Temple Balsall church before her death.[1] Henry VIII's commissioners had cast their eyes on the lead covering the roof, and it is a fair assumption that this was stripped as the whole roof needed rebuilding by the time of Lady Anne, as also the bell turret. She made her will in 1663, 'written all in my own Hand without advice of Council'. She made a great many generous bequests including £100 a year to endow a preaching ministry at Balsall 'to the end of the World' and £500 towards the repair of St Mary's church. She was then advised that her estate would not meet the costs of her debts and her bequests, and the above £100 was reduced to an annual £50, and the £500 to £200.[2] In the event, the Long Itchington estate was sold to defray her over-generous dispositions.

From watercolour drawings of the church (fig.24) after Lady Anne's restoration and before Scott's work of 1849, we can be sure of what she did.[3] A comparison with the description of 1541 reveals the scale of the work she financed. It is considerable, and presumably reflects the degree of ruination after more than a hundred years' neglect and possibly vandalism.

24 St Mary's, Temple Balsall, from the east, pre-1849. Note the steep pitch of the roof, barely clearing the tops of the side windows. (Warwick CRO PV TEM (chu 3a). Drawn by David Warren from an original in the Aylesford Collection, Birmingham Reference Library.)

25 Watercolour of the church from the south west, 1804. (Warwick CRO DR 9B 23/76/1.)

All aspects of the church except the north elevation are shown in these drawings; the number of windows and their individual lights, together with the style of tracery, appear to be identical with what Scott's restoration has left us today. It is fair to assume that the north windows also correspond.

The description left by Henry VIII's commissioners gives large five-light windows at both east and west ends, as today, but it is the windows of the south side and of the chancel which do not correspond.

It is possible that the east and west gables were the main surviving structures, with perhaps some lower courses of walling and buttresses between.

The heavy, disproportionately large, bell-tower of the watercolours agrees so poorly with the 1541 description of 'the steeple—a very little one' that it must certainly be of the 1663 build. (This was the only major change made, justifiably, by Scott.)

26 Lady Anne Holbourne's font, 1663. The Rev. Thomas Ward visited Temple Balsall in 1830 and included the church in his report (BL Addl. MS 2965). The stone font had a circumference of 7 feet 6 inches, with foliated carvings on the outside. This fits the above font perfectly. (The 1541 font was of timber, lined with lead with a small bar over.) It must have been ejected from the church by Scott in his 1849 restoration, and it stood in one or another local garden until it was restored to the church in about 1986.

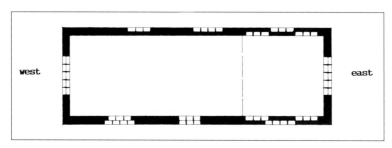

27 Diagram showing a comparison between the church windows and their lights in the 1541 survey (the inner lights) and those left after Lady Anne's restoration of 1663 (the outer lights).

Reverting to Lady Anne's bequests, she left her mother, the Duchess, who survived her by three years, £200 to buy a ring or jewel 'as a poor remembrance of my Love and Duty to her', and £100 each to the poor of the parishes of Balsall and Long Itchington, amongst many other bequests.

Lady Katherine's Will

Lady Katherine followed her sister's example in writing her own will—'wrought with my own hand and having no skill in law phrases'. She asks for her body to be buried in the chancel of 'Linsell' [Lilleshall] church where her husband lies. She sets aside £1,000 for her funeral, wishing that her neighbours, knights, ladies and gentlemen, who shall be at her burial, should have 'mourning things' of the best sort, for such as are of quality and her friends. To others of lower degree, 'à la mode scarves', and to the 'worser', ribbons. Her most substantial bequest was £1,000 in gold to Prince Rupert to buy a ring 'or what he pleases as a widow's mite to express my humble thankfulness for former honour he did me'. What this honour was is not known.[4]

There follow many smaller legacies, in the form of money or jewels, and the residue then was to go to several churches to buy plate or ornaments: Lichfield Cathedral, Trentham and Lilleshall churches. She adds as an afterthought, Balsall church 'to be another to have part of my money left as the other named churches'. This first will was dated 27 January 1668.[5]

She made two codicils to this in October 1670, increasing her legacies to

28 Impression of the Corporation seal of the Governors of Temple Balsall. Legend: *sigillum dominae Catherinae Leveson de Balsall in comitatu Waricii*. Lady Katherine is depicted holding her escutcheon and nursing one of the children, in reference to her founding the boys' school. (Warwick CRO CR 112 Ba/180, September 1702 [no pagination]: Mr. Bromley is to be paid £6 14s. for printing the Act of Parliament and cutting the Corporation seal of the Hospital.) (For the Act of Parliament, Queen Anne, 30 December 1701-2, see Appendix I[a].)

her various servants, and in the following February returned to the task. This latter is so long and complex as hardly to be described as a codicil; it is this section which is of the greatest importance to Temple Balsall.

Amongst many dispositions of property and new legacies, she left £100 to the town of Trentham to set up a trust for the schooling of poor children till they could be put out as apprentices. Some of the new clauses deal with what she has recently received from her mother's (the Duchess') will, chiefly the manor of Foxley (Northants), and she also remembers that she has not yet disposed of the lordship of Balsall. Valuable items such as a silver warming pan, silver perfuming pan, silver [coffee] cans with the duchess' arms upon them, abound amongst many jewelled ornaments. One clause concerns some of her clothes, some of which she bequeaths '… but not my petticoat set with pearls to anybody', and she declared that 'I will have none of my clothes sold except old silver lace'.

As regards Foxley and Balsall, she states that it is her intention to dispose of them to pious and charitable uses, and sets up a trust of six worthy men to carry out her wish that all the rents and profits from Foxley should be used to provide £120 a year for 12 poor widows, six in the parishes within Foxley manor, three in Lilleshall

29 Lady Katherine's gift of church plate to Temple Balsall: silver-gilt chalice, 1678, same maker as flagon, height 9¾ in., weight 20 oz. 10 dwt; silver-gilt paten by the same maker, height 1⁷⁄₈ in., weight 16 oz. 15 dwt.; silver-gilt flagon, 1678, inscribed below 'Ex dono Katherine Leveson'. Maker's mark F.S.; height 14¾ in., weight 86 oz.

30 Katherine, fourth and last surviving daughter of Sir Robert Dudley Knt and Lady Alicia Dudley his wife. She was relict of Sir Richard Leveson, Knight of the Bath of Trentham. (From the original picture in the Collection of the Duke of Sutherland at Trentham Hall.)

and three in Trentham. Out of the £10 was to be provided one gown of grey cloth, on the breast of which the letters 'K.L.' were to be set in blue cloth. The gowns were to be worn constantly as a condition of the charity. One hundred pounds were to be used to set 10 poor boys out of the same parishes apprentice to some honest and lawful calling. After these wishes have been met, £40 is to be employed annually on repairs to the Beauchamp Chapel at St Mary's church, Warwick, 'where my ancestors are interred' (the Dudley connections).

This last bequest she wished to be administered by the mayor of Warwick, and William Dugdale (later Sir William), and it still today is so administered by their successors and descendants, the mayor and Sir William Dugdale. The annuity, known as the Foxley Charity, is commemorated by a marble plaque on the north wall of the chapel; it states that the tombs in the chapel were 'much blemisht by consuming time and more by the rude hands of impious people', and in danger of 'utter ruine', that she gave £50 in her lifetime, and the £40 bequest from the Foxley estate. It was William Dugdale the antiquary, author of *The Antiquities of Warwickshire*, who shrewdly drew the attention of this wealthy widow to the state of the chapel. Any residue from the £40 was to go to the poor Brethren of Lord Leycester's Hospital in Warwick, but there seems to have been little left over for the Brethren over the years.

A curious clause refers to 'the poor boys that is in my house'. She gives them £10 apiece, to be paid on her death. This is over and above what she has bequeathed to bind them as apprentices. It seems that she took them into her house at Trentham perhaps to serve as, say, boot-boys, until they were old enough to be sent out to be bound as apprentices.

She came at last to Temple Balsall, and it is evident that she had given this project much thought.

Lady Katherine and Temple Balsall

Following the recovery of Temple Balsall by the two sisters in 1656 a Court of Survey was held in May 1657 and in October of that year the full Court Leet and Court Baron were held, and the roll survives.[6] Surprisingly the name of Sir Richard Leveson, Knight of the Bath, appears first in the heading of the roll, followed by his wife, Lady Katherine and the Lady Anne, as lords of the manor. This must be a mistake for though Sir Richard had been called, presumably to make a deposition, in the recovery, the title to the manor was firmly settled on the sisters. On Lady Anne's death in 1663, Lady Katherine bought her three shares of Temple Balsall, and so in her will, as full and undisputed owner, she declared: 'To the honour of God and to the pious and charitable uses hereafter herein mentioned, I do hereby give and devise all that my said Manor or Lordship of Balsall to ...' and

31   The hatchment of Lady Katherine Leveson (died 1674), displaying the Dudley lion rampant, and the three laurel leaves for Leveson. It is the oldest surviving datable example in the county. Cf. P. Summers (ed.), *Hatchments in Britain 1: Northamptonshire, Warwickshire and Worcestershire* (Chichester, 1975). It hangs in the Old Hall. In 1794 a Mr. Wigan was paid 10 gns for painting the King's, Lady Leveson's and Lady Anne Holbourne's Arms for the church. Carriage from London 1s. 6d. (Warwick CRO CR 112 Ba/181, item 31.)

there follow the names of 11 trustees, landed gentry, three from Warwickshire, one from Cheshire and seven from Staffordshire. The list closes with the additional name of Thomas Evetts of Balsall, her bailiff there, whom she includes with the last six, under the title 'gentlemen'. She evidently thought highly of him, for earlier in her will she directed that he should have two years' salary on her death.[7]

The trustees were to erect a house of stone or brick as near to the church as convenient as a hospital or almshouse, of such height, largeness and quantity as suitable, with backsides, gardens and easements as convenient. On some part of the house her name and gift was to be publicly displayed. Immediately after the house was finished 20 poor widows or poor spinsters of good lives were to be installed, to remain there for the rest of their lives, the poorest and 'such as be lame and in greatest distress' to be always preferred. They were to have eight pounds a year in money and one gown of grey cloth a year with the letters 'K.L.' on the breast. Any who refused to wear this was to be ejected from the house. These were the same gowns as those specified for the widows of Foxley, Lilleshall and Trentham, who forfeited their benefit if they refused to wear them.

If there were not enough poor women in Balsall to qualify for the charity, then the numbers might be made up from Long Itchington, Trentham and Lilleshall. A

29 The church and Old Hall, Temple Balsall, 1838. (From the *Gentlemen's Magazine*, September 1838.)

minister was to be found, to read the Scriptures twice a day and to instruct the women for the good of their souls, and he was to have £20 a year for this service. The rest of the rents and profits were to be used for repairs, expenses and taxation. Thomas Evetts was to receive these moneys, out of which he was to pay the minister and the poor women, to be the overseer of the building and to have £10 a year for himself for his pains. He was to be accountable to the trustees, who were to elect his successor after his death. The poor women were to be elected by the trustees; if there were to be some notorious misbehaviour by any of the women, the trustees had the power to remove them. Lady Katherine signed this long codicil on 21 February 1671.

* * *

Yet another codicil followed in the December, giving her god-daughter Mary Lucy £1,000 towards her marriage portion.

* * *

A final codicil was added on 18 December 1673, requiring the minister who was to read the Scriptures, *also* to teach 20 of the poorest boys in Balsall, constantly until they were fit to be apprenticed. This duty was to be considered as paid for by the £20, and he was not to take anything from the parents of the boys.

So there she had laid the foundation of the set-up in Temple Balsall as it is more than three hundred years later. She died the next year.

* * *

That Lady Katherine's life had its lighter moments may be inferred from the following recipe:[8]

Lady K Leveson's Bones

2lbs Savoy Biscuits
1lb Macaroons
1lb Ratifias
1 pint Brandy
1 pint Sherry
12 yolks Eggs

* * *

A prayer for the almswomen to say in thankfulness for their good fortune, suggests that a spirit of deference, of consciousness of their position as charitable subjects, was thought to become them. As will appear in a later chapter, they seem to have been treated well, even generously, perhaps as long as they knew their place.

The Almswomen's Prayer[9]

O only Eternal Omnipotent Incomprehensible and most gracious Lord,
who of thy mere goodness, free grace and Compassion,
to thy poor creature man, for the increase of his Faith and
Dependence on thee, and true obedience to thee,
Hast in all ages given some signal Testimonies of thy bounties,
and inspired Eminent servants of thine to exemplarie works
of Pietie and Charitie, Wee poor creatures which abundantly tast
of this thy benificence, do most humbly beseech thee make us
with enlarged soules and truly zealous affections, adore and extoll
thy glorious majesty. For all thy bounties, Particularly those
derived to us by our renowned Benefactress, whereby wee being released
from the exigencies of poverty and necessity of carkinge and labouring
for bodily sustenance, our soules may be enlarged in fervent Hallelujahs
to thee our gracious God, our lives addicted through piety to
thy faithful service, our actions regulated to the decent orders of
our Societie, and wee thereby and by thy especiall influence, the
better prepared with oyle in our Lamps to meet the Bridegroom in the
day of our disolution. And this wee most humbly begg of thy free
grace, Through the merits and intercession of thy son our Saviour
Jesus Christ, to whome with thee and thy Holy Spirit, bee all
honour, glory, dominion and praise now and ever.
Amen

Chapter 13

The Hospital, Schoolhouse and Master's House

Lady Katherine betrayed a certain urgency in her will, perhaps realising that her days were numbered; the trustees were asked to organise the conveyance of the manor 'with all convenient speed', and after the erection and finishing of the almshouse, the almswomen were to be installed 'immediately'. She died in fact in 1674, and the undated draft agreement between the builder and the trustees specified a completion date of 1 October 1676.[1] In the event, the first poor women were admitted in 1679, which, considering the size of the undertaking, seems remarkably expeditious.

Sir William Bromley of Baginton, Knight of the Bath, and Thomas Evetts, gentleman, the Bailiff of Balsall, represented the trustees. The builder was William Hurlbutt of Warwick, also accorded the title of gentleman. He had built the Market Hall (now the County Museum in Warwick market place) in 1670. With his brother Roger, William had been employed at Warwick Castle from 1669 to 1678 on the wainscoting of the Great Hall and the Cedar Room, as they were exceptionally skilled carpenters. They were also capable of designing buildings, and came to be styled 'architects'.[2]

Agreement with the Builder

Hurlbutt covenanted to build with stone and good brick an almshouse, with a school-house and Master's house 'in the form of a street', each range to be 122 feet long and 19 feet wide within the walls, for the dwellings of 20 poor women besides the school house and Master's house; the specifications are given in great detail, and one in particular is noteworthy; the walls of the almshouses were to be eight feet high from the surface of the ground to the wall-plate (the eaves). There were to be five compartments in each of the two ranges, each with a partition wall (to serve as two dwellings) and each to have two little dormer windows for the bedrooms above.

The doors and windows were to be set off with a border of well-wrought stone, and each range to have a pediment ornamented with a medallion or in similar 'commendable fashion'. The rooms were to be well plastered and the bedrooms to be ceiled.

The Master's (Schoolmaster's) House

The Master's house was to be 34 feet in length, 17 feet within the walls, and, in strong contrast with the almshouses, to be 19 feet from the ground to the wall-plate, in other words, to tower over them as though to emphasise their difference in status. There was to be a bell surmounting the Master's house, to call the women to prayer. The doors and windows were to have similar borders of stone to the almshouses, and the main door to have an escutcheon with Lady Katherine's arms and a memorial of her gift. The flooring of the ground floor was to be of good brick as in the almshouses (except that the parlour floor was to be boarded as the bedroom floors of the women). This is referred to in Hurlbutt's bill as 'The Scoolemaster's House and Kittchin', which with the schoolhouse make up the space on the north side between the ranges of almshouses. (For a list of the Masters, see Appendix VI.)

33 The Master's House, north side, before rebuilding. (Warwick CRO PV Tem. Gen 3. From an original in the Aylesford Collection, Birmingham Reference Library.)

34 The Court after the almshouses were rebuilt.

The Schoolhouse

A mere three lines of the agreement deal with the schoolhouse (which is little more than a room), and those are concerned entirely with its furnishings, but as it still survives, though engulfed in the 19th-century rebuild of the Master's house, its outer appearance and location can be shown with confidence as on page 54. There was to be a handsome reading desk of oak for the Master, and the whole school (that is, the single room) to have benches about the walls and oak panelling above them 30 inches deep. Low forms were to be fixed before the benches. Three of these 'forms' survive, though no longer fixed, and the benches and panelling above still exist, as does the Master's desk. A small kitchen completed the tiny schoolhouse, an afterthought in Lady Katherine's will, and seemingly in the planning of the whole complex.

There was to be a seven-foot high enclosing wall, with two stone pillars surmounted by stone balls, and a pair of iron gates. Two 'houses of office' and two wells with 'handsome well-made' pumps completed the plans for the Hospital.

35   The Court, Temple Balsall: drawing by David Warren, 1993. This shows the Master's House before the 19th-century re-build, based on contemporary watercolours, and the almshouses before their partial rebuild in the 1720s, based on the specifications of William Hurlbutt, the original builder. This is how the Court may have looked when the first almswomen came in 1679. Note the low height of the almshouses compared with the Master's House.

36   The old boys' school, now called the Prayer Room as it was once so used by the Dames in bad weather. From Easter to September teas were served to the public in this room for many years. It is sandwiched between the Master's House on the left and the east range of the Court on the right. In 1998 it was converted into the Master's Study.

Hurlbutt's Bill[3]

He submitted this at Easter 1679 'at which time The women came there to Dwell'. The ten houses (each to house two women) came to £500, that is £50 per house. The schoolmaster's house and the schoolhouse together came to £300, and the total bill of £960 was made up by the paving, walling and so on. An additional bill of £50 was claimed for masons', carpenters' and bricklayers' work and cost of materials (he had had to buy in an extra £20 worth of timber, on top of what he was allowed from the estate, for the woodwork in the houses, and to fire his bricks). The cost of the Master's house does not seem to have survived.

37 William Hurlbutt's bill for the building of the almshouses and schoolhouse at Easter 1679, at which time 'The women came there to dwell'.

Almshouses

There are often structural resemblances in these buildings, chiefly occasioned by the need for economy, especially the use of the terrace form of building, the use of the roof space with dormer windows to serve as bedrooms, and single entrances for two dwellings. Overleaf are three examples:

1. CHIPPING CAMPDEN: almshouses built in 1612 by Sir Baptist Hicks. These are taller than many but have the terrace form, the dormer windows and single entrances serving two dwellings.

2. STONELEIGH: ten almshouses built in 1594 by Lady Alice Leigh, Lady Katherine's great grandmother (see Chapter 11). The date is carved over the central doorway. Again the range is terraced, the height to the eaves is 15 feet, and the roof space, with

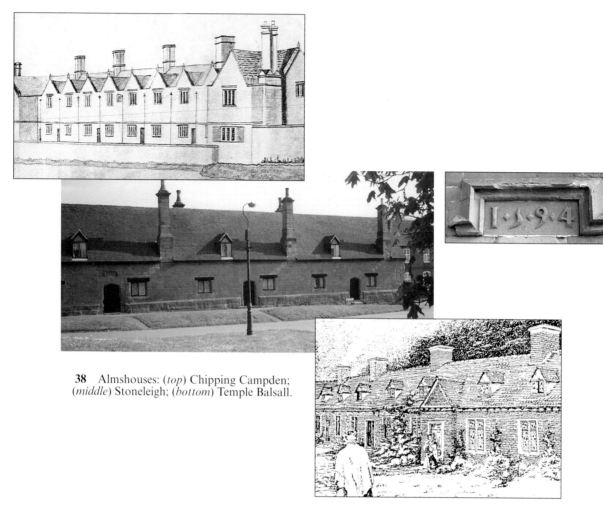

38 Almshouses: (*top*) Chipping Campden;
(*middle*) Stoneleigh; (*bottom*) Temple Balsall.

dormer windows, is used for the bedrooms; the outside measurement from front to back is 20 feet. Each doorway leads to a passage which has an entrance on both sides.

3.TEMPLE BALSALL: this is an impression of the original range before the re-building and heightening of 1725, using Hurlbutt's specifications, and assuming that the style and ornamentation were similar to what is seen today, for much still agrees with Hurlbutt—the stone borders round doors and windows, and the central pediment with medallion. The height from the ground level to the eaves was originally 8 feet. The terracing, dormers, and single door for two apartments all resemble Stoneleigh; the inside measurement from front to back is 19 feet. It is possible that Hurlbutt used the Stoneleigh range as a basis for a more extensive, more decorative group of buildings, for Lord Leigh, one of the Governors of Temple Balsall, would be well aware of the history of the almshouses in Stoneleigh village and their connection with the Leigh family.

Chapter 14

The Women came there to Dwell

The need for almshouses was the result of a number of social upheavals. The monasteries had played a part in caring for the sick and infirm, and Henry VIII's Dissolution removed this source of help at a stroke. The survey of Arbury Priory at the time of the Dissolution showed that there were 'six impotent persons and children' dependent there.[1] The low regard in which this group was held by the surveyors is evident from the way they are lumped indistinguishably together. The Civil War of the next century doubtless added to the number of poor widows, whose plight could be compounded by fear of accusations of witchcraft, until the Witchcraft Act of 1736 which repealed the already obsolete law condemning a witch to death, thus reflecting the growing disbelief in witchcraft among the educated classes (though belief probably persisted much longer in rural areas). Persons of wealth and good conscience, no doubt hoping to ensure their salvation by good works, might set up almshouses to alleviate distress, as did Alice Leigh, Lady Katherine's great-grandmother, with her ten alms-

39 'Swimming' a witch, late 16th century. (From L.F. Salzman, *England in Tudor Times*, 1922.)

houses at Stoneleigh.[2] As she lived to see the fourth generation of her descendants, it is not impossible that she might have seen Lady Katherine as a child. The aged lady could well have become a legend in the family, and been in Lady Katherine's mind when she made her will.

The first women to be admitted to the hospital or almshouse of Temple Balsall were elected at a meeting of the trustees on 10 October 1678 in Coventry.[3] Their names are recorded as follows:

Joan Berry	Joan Phillips
Margaret Corbet	Alice Chesterton
Anne Watson	Jane Ballamye
Isabel Gruby	Dennis [*sic*] Rainbow
Ann Davis	Ann Michell
Mary Barnacle	Ann Ditchfield
Elizabeth Morrice	Mary Watson
Ursula Ashford	Katherine Melodye
Susannah Hanks	Bridget Phipps
Sarah Titmus	Isabel Barnacle

It is not revealed whether the two Watsons and two Barnacles are related. Three were evidently near their end, for Susannah died on 20 May 1679, a mere month after her admission at Easter (20 April 1679), and Elizabeth Morrice followed her the next day, while Ursula Ashford held out until 20 October that year.

The list of deaths and admissions continues until 1835, then resumes after the register of poor boys. Some women lived to a great age. In 1783, when it was not usual to record the ages of the women, Elizabeth Boston died on 26 January aged 108, and Elizabeth Page followed her on 5 February aged 94 (remarkably enough to merit recording). Mary Green died aged 97 in 1810, after 51 years in the Hospital and

40   Dames in the Court. (Photo: *Birmingham Post*, undated.)

Mary Edwards had lived 53 years there before her death in 1820 at the age of ninety. More sombre events are recorded in the entries 'Mary Woodward was expelled August 6th 1789', and 'Mary Smith destroyed herself 7th November 1794'.

The need for this succour for distressed old women continued into the next century as is clear from a letter to the trustees about Mary Powner; it was dated at Trentham 17 October 1850, probably written by her vicar, who recommended her as a 65-year-old widow, a religious woman of exemplary life and conversation. He realises that 'it will be a bitter thing to leave a place in which she has dwelt longer than I, and I have called it my home sixty years ago'. He has to undertake the cost of her removal 'for she has not a sixpence in store', and he wondered if her 'trifles of furniture' might be carried by boat (along the canal, that is, for economy). Mary 'pleads earnestly for time to go the rounds of her children and pay them a last visit'.[4]

Needy women from Trentham, Lilleshall and Long Itchington were eligible for the almshouses if there happened to be vacancies not filled by Balsall women, but it is clear from this letter that some might regard it as sorrowful exile from their old homes. In later years, such elected women were granted a pension rather than being transferred to Balsall.

A list of the rules and orders to be observed by the almswomen now hangs in the Master's Study (the former Schoolroom). Printed in heavy black type, the whole is now blackened with age. It has a rather daunting aspect, but seems reasonable in its provisions as long as it was interpreted in a humane way.

For the Act of Parliament passed in 1701 to formalise the organisation and procedures at the Hospital see Appendix III.

41 Extract from a letter supporting Mary Powner's application to become an almswoman at the Old Hall.

RULES & ORDERS
TO BE OBSERVED IN THE
HOSPITAL OF LADY
KATHERINE LEVESON
at
TEMPLE BALSALL

I That every Almswoman, unless prevented by illness, attend Public Prayers daily, Morning and Evening, either at the Church, or in a Room within the Hospital, to be appointed by the Master, and habited in the Dress provided by the Governors.

II That no Almswoman be allowed to absent herself from the Hospital for more than one day, or to keep another inmate in her dwelling for more than the same period, without special permission obtained from the Master of the Hospital.

III That no Almswoman appear abroad except in the Dress provided for her by the Governors.

IV That every Almswoman be particularly careful to keep her House, Stair-case and everything belonging to her in a state of cleanliness, and that she also in her turn clean the Prayer-Room and Court.

V That each Almswoman, when required by the Master shall in her turn attend during the night upon any of the other Almswomen who are ill.

VI That the Master of the Hospital have power to fine the Almswomen in a sum not exceeding one shilling per week for breach of Rules; and that upon a written Certificate of the fine being given by him to the Bailiff, the money shall be deducted from her weekly allowance, and accounted for by the Governors.

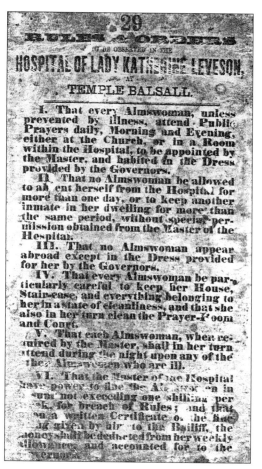

42 Almswomen's regulations.

It is clear that there were problems both for the authorities and the almswomen, especially with regard to the health of the women and attendance on them when sick. In June 1704 the Order Book notes that 'Some almswomen are absent from the Hospital with their relations upon pretence of want of health, to take care of them. Some one of the younger and more healthy [women] to be appointed to attend on the sick

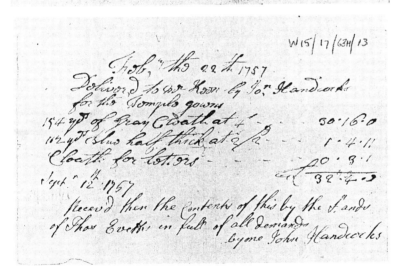

43 Bills for the making of 28 gowns for the women, at 2s. 6d. per gown. Materials included whalebone and canvas; total cost: £38 0s. 4½d. The initials 'KL' were applied to the breast of the gowns in blue.[17]

and impotent'. By 1708, *two* nurses were to have their salaries (40s. each) for the past two years.[5]

In 1715 Widow Truelove was to be appointed nurse for the next year. Subsequent entries hint that hers cannot have been the most soothing hand for the fevered brow, for in 1724 there is the 'complaint that Widow Truelove continues to behave herself in a turbulent manner, scolding and swearing to the disturbance of the peace … notwithstanding repeated admonitions'. Half her salary was to be cut, and Widow Loome appointed nurse in her place. It does not appear that she was expelled, however.[6]

44 One of the original Dames' tables, of which a number survive. These were supplied by the Governors for the use of the almswomen in their rooms.

It is surprising that almost a hundred years elapsed before the Governors decided to appoint a matron. In 1774, Mrs. Susannah Harrold was to be appointed Matron from Michaelmas at a salary of £20 a year. She was to 'superintend the poor women that they behave according to the rules, and secondly to examine them each day as regards their health, and see that the nurses do their duty in giving proper attendance upon the sick'. Two inscriptions in Temple Balsall church commemorate Mrs. Harrold: one on a stone on the floor—'Susannah Harrold died 20 May 1800 aged 74 years, matron of this hospital for 26 years'—and a wall marble—'Sacred to the memory of Mrs Susannah Harrold, relict of the Reverend Sharman Harrold, died 20 July 1800 aged 74 ...'. She served until August 1800, when Mrs. Frances Harrold (?a relation) was appointed in her place as she had died.[7]

45   Matron's House: the east wing of the Court.

By 1730 there were 30 old women, and the two nurses were to have 50 shillings each, for this year there had been more illness than usual.[8] The 1981 excavation at the Old Hall (see below pp.84-91) revealed a considerable number of medicine phials, whole and in sherds; they were presumed to have come from treating the sick almswomen, and this conjecture was confirmed by the entry for 1776,[9] when Mr. Bree of Solihull was to be asked to attend and find medicine for the old women for five guineas a year, and if he decline, some other apothecary was to be found; this is admittedly later than the date when the artefacts were thrown into the cellar, but no doubt continued a custom.

Further proof that the welfare of the old women was not neglected is shown towards the end of the 18th century.[10] On account of the scarcity and dearness of provisions in the last quarter of the century, the old women were allowed an extra 30 shillings on top of their usual annual 40 shillings, with an extra 9d. a week on top, and in 1801 the Bailiff was instructed

46 A resident, Mrs. Penny Gardner, dressed as a Dame, during the *Son et Lumière* event (1985). She is wearing the bonnet, gown and summer shawl of thin black/grey check cotton. For winter the shawls were thick woollen black/red check. From 1921 the Master could allow the Dames to wear ordinary clothes away from the Hospital. In 1962 all compulsion was removed, though some liked to wear the dress outside, feeling that it distinguished them.

to procure a cow for the old women's benefit.[11] By this date there was a fairly steady 30 women in residence.

The second Rule presented a particular temptation. Understandably the old women would relish visits from their relations, who would doubtless enjoy a brief holiday at the Court (the name by which the almshouse complex was and is popularly called). But the Governors took a very serious view of extended visits; in 1707 the Master complained that 'the poor women do entertain their relations there', and the order went forth that if they did not reform upon a second warning the Bailiff was to stop 6d. a week from their pay, and on the third warning they were to be expelled. Again, later, the women residing in the Hospital were to be forbidden to allow their relations 'to lodge and remain with them under pain of the Governors' displeasure'.[12]

The opening years of the 20th century saw a surprising new problem, drunkenness amongst some of the Dames. Perhaps the availability of cheap gin proved too strong a temptation; also the more active women were probably more mobile, for

47   Dames going to Evensong. (Photo: Temple Balsall Archive)

regulations about leaving bicycles in the Court began to appear. In 1902 a special rule was introduced—no Dame should keep spirits in her room without the permission of the Master. Two years later the Governors declared that it was the duty of the Master to report any cases of drunkenness and to warn the offenders of the danger of expulsion. Accordingly Dame Charlotte Ball appeared before the Governors and was admonished and warned. A second offence led to her expulsion. The same year (1904) Dame Gittins also offended and was warned, but soon after was found drunk on the road between Knowle and Temple Balsall. She was also expelled. (Yet the Governors were liberal-minded about the proper uses of alcohol as they sanctioned medicinal doses of whisky, brandy and port for Dames in need.) Other problems might sometimes arise as in the case of the deranged Widow Whitmore who had to be sent off to Stafford Lunatic Asylum. Later (1844), candidates for the hospital had to produce a certificate that they were not subject to fits or of unsound mind.[13]

But these were exceptional cases; their offences led to their appearance in the records. It would be regrettable if we were left with the impression that the Court was peopled with a crowd of drunken viragos. The majority of the scores of women who passed through the Court over the years remained anonymous except for their receptions and departures on their death—inoffensive and respectable women such as Mary Powner (above, p.59) and Joan Miles. Some admittedly were illiterate, for it was part of Matron's duties to read and write their letters for them, but others evidently passed their time in reading, for in 1852 the Governors voted £10 towards the lending library

48 Some of the many Dames' graves in the churchyard, marked with small headstones.

in the Hospital, though when in 1888 Mr. Short, the Master, asked for a donation for the lending library and the erection of a reading room, the Governors gave £2, but refused the request for a reading room.[14]

Old Joan

Amongst the many surviving records of Temple Balsall is the will of Joan Miles, spinster.[15] She dictated it in the presence of Thomas Evetts, the Bailiff, and Mary Evetts, his wife[16] on 14 August 1726. Perhaps it was on her death-bed, but she declares herself to be 'of sound and disposing mind', and certainly her declared wishes bear this out. The handwriting is that of the Bailiff, and towards the end she refers to 'my Master Evetts' two sons'. The will is endorsed 'Old Joan's will'.

So here was an old servant of the Bailiff, who had found a refuge for her old age in the Court, a few hundred yards from her place of employment at the Old Hall. Her will bespeaks a just and rational mind, in full control of her affairs. A doubtless frugal and disciplined life had left her with almost £11 in money to dispose of; of this £5 'and no more' is to be expended on her funeral. The remaining money is shared out amongst no less than 18 legatees, chiefly nieces and nephews, 11 of them at twelvepence apiece. Her sister Alice is her chief beneficiary, with 40 shillings for herself and 10 shillings each for her six children.

Her clothes include seven 'shifts' (linen undergarments), a best 'suit' of linen, and one of wool, the sole luxurious item being a 'silver-laced' petticoat. In furnishings

49   Some of the Dames' graves in the meadow graveyard; Eliza Lewis is the last one at the top.

she leaves a blanket, feather-bed and bolster and sheets, and the curtains at the windows and round her bed. She has some small items of furniture, a chest, two coffers and a cupboard. She carefully itemises her bellows, chopping-knife, her loom, cooler and the bigger barrel, the last three of which she leaves to her sister Alice for her life, then to Alice's daughter, along with her 'best pot'; the word 'loom' can mean, in dialect, an 'open vessel', and it is here itemised amongst the dairy equipment, but since she also bequeathes, immediately above, to her niece Elizabeth, one shift and a 'Wallet of linnen cloath', it is more likely that it was a weaving loom, and that Old Joan wove the linen for her shifts. Perhaps Alice's life was also moving towards its close. Three pewter dishes and a pewter porringer were separately bequeathed, and she concluded with the wish that 'my Master Evetts two sons, Mr Barlow and Mr William' should each have a pair of white gloves (?to wear at her funeral, white being a token of mourning at that time).

In all, she seems to depart on good terms with the world, and probably the world with her.

* * *

Care of the Dames

Dame Eliza Lewis

20 July 1919: The Bailiff writes to Nurse Reader: 'By all means get dark glasses for those Dames you consider require them and also get the air cushion for Dame Lewis ...'

22 August 1919:   The Bailiff writes to Dr. Whatley (physician to the Dames): 'Would Dame Lewis be better moved to the ground floor to enable her to go out in a wheelchair?—but the stone floors on the ground floor should be taken into account ...'

4 September 1919:   The Bailiff to Nurse Reader: asks her to let him know the amount of whisky, brandy and port that she has in stock for the Dames ...

25 September 1919: It is decided to move Dame Lewis downstairs ...

9 November 1920:   The Bailiff to Dr. Whatley: 'Dame Lewis is now quite helpless

50 Eliza Lewis: trial outing in the wheelchair, 1918, with attendant nurse, two almswomen, and possibly Nurse Reader behind. (Photo: Temple Balsall Archive)

and cannot be left day or night—should she be removed to the Infirmary at Solihull?'

18 November 1920:   The Bailiff writes to Mr. Fairbairn, the Master, in much the same terms as above …

20 November 1920:   The Bailiff writes to Mr. Richard Lant, a member of the Estates Committee; he quotes Dr. Whatley as saying that Dame Lewis is suffering from rheumatoid arthritis and is getting worse, needs a nurse day and night, and her present 8 shillings a week is not enough for her support. The Doctor recommends that she go to the Infirmary as she is likely to become bedridden …

22 November 1920:   The Bailiff writes to Nurse Reader: 'Any Dame who has paid one shilling in preference to sitting up at night with Dame Lewis is to have her shilling returned, but this does not alter the Rule but is done as an act of grace …

30 November 1920:   The Bailiff presses Mr. Fairbairn for a decision about Dame Lewis …

11 December 1920:   It was decided that Dame Lewis is to go 'on Monday next' …

7 February 1921:   The Bailiff to Nurse: 'You can order the tombstone for Dame Lewis' …

And so she came 'home' to Temple Balsall. Her grave is in the overflow graveyard on the slope down to the brook, the last Dame to be buried near the church before the cemetery was closed and the new one at Rabbit Lane opened.

It is noteworthy that Dame Lewis was only 57 when she died. Her grave is at the end of a row of six, all of Dames. Moving along the row, her neighbours are: Mary

51   The headstone to Eliza Lewis.

Wheeler, died 20 October 1920, aged 95; Harriet Tandy, died 9 July 1920, aged 90; Mary Ann Fitter, died 18 May 1919, aged 89; Ann Smith, died 19 January 1916, aged 91; and Sarah Livingstone, died 26 April 1915, aged 68. The regulation age of 60 for admission to the Hospital (which still applies today) must have been waived in Eliza's case, perhaps because of her condition, since she was admitted in 1914, when she would have been 50 years old.[18]

52   Dames' outing—date and location unknown. (Photo: Temple Balsall Archive)

Chapter 15

The Boys came to School

On Tuesday 13 May 1679 the first 20 poor boys came to school at Temple Balsall.[1] They were:

	Left		Left
Nicholas Edwards	20 Jun 81	John Smith	9 Nov 82
Thomas Earl	20 Apr 81	Thomas Bissell	2 Jul82
James Arch	2 Aug 80	Samuel Hunt	7 Aug 82
John Smith	7 Apr ?85	Edward Mathewes	20 Mar 83
Joseph Anstey	12 Oct 83	Joseph Bennet	12 Oct 83
William Hamon	4 Dec 82	John Spiers	12 Jun 80
John Bradnock	26 Apr 84	Thomas Badams	10 Feb 79 [sic]
Richard Peyton	23 Apr 80	John Ward	21 Oct 80
John Chatterley	16 Feb 81	Henry Saul	30 Jul 79
William Brown	11 Apr 82	William Wall	30 Nov 79

The names do not suggest that any were brothers, unless perhaps the two John Smiths, for it could happen that if the elder child were sickly, a second might be given the same name as a precaution.

Half the boys stayed for three years or more, some as long as four. Exceptionally, John Bradnock (five years) and John Smith (six years) continued their schooling even longer. Just under half stayed only for two years or less, considerably less in the case of Henry Saul (two months) and William Wall (six months). Leavers' places were soon taken by new boys; the three earliest leavers were the two boys mentioned above and Richard Peyton who left on 23 April 1680; the vacancies were filled by Moses Bird (30 January 1680), William Ward (3 March 1680) and William Berry (3 April 1680).

No attempt had been made in this country to teach elementary reading and writing to the mass of the people until the foundation of charity schools such as Lady Katherine set up in her will. The grammar schools had long provided a secondary

53   The boys' schoolroom, with the Master's desk and the benches round the walls. The corner cupboard was provided in 1818 for bibles and prayer books. Note: the cushions on the benches are modern! (Photo: Max Ellerslie.) 'The School house is to have a handsome reading pue [*sic*] and desk of wainscot …' (Warwick CRO CR 112/177/1).

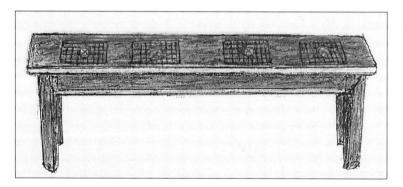

54   Schoolboys' form, once fixed before the benches in the boys' schoolroom. Three of these survive, 6 feet long, 1 foot wide, with four diagrams scribed on the surface, evidently for the use of four boys.

55   Diagram—one of four inscribed on each schoolboy's bench. A similar form, with diagrams, is to be found at Temple Newsam (Yorks.), once a Templar property which did not pass to the Hospitallers. (Information from Mrs. Jean Watson Williams.)

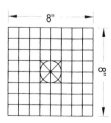

education based on Latin, but these were not for the labouring classes, rather the sons of yeomen, small gentry and the like. The State did nothing until the 19th and 20th centuries. From the hundred per cent uptake of places over many years it is clear that the schooling was valued at Balsall.

56 Bedlam's End with the old *Tom o' Bedlam Inn*, long discontinued as an inn. The area is now known as Chadwick End, along with Chadwick End proper. The Dame's School may have been in this row.

After the register of boys admitted, there seems to be no reference to the school in the records until, in 1744, the Governors found it necessary to state their wishes about admission.[2] Concerning 'the qualification of boys to be admitted into the School', they ordered that ' for the future no boy regularly [that is, according to the rule] recommended shall be refused by the Master so soon as he can read his primmer by spelling'. This sounds as though it was in response to a particular case of refusal. But where would the boys acquire this qualification, however rudimentary it seems?

It is impossible to say. The setting up of a Dame's School in Bedlam's End was proposed by the Governors in 1841, with a passing reference to a Sunday School 'with already nearly 50 children'.[3] But this is a hundred years later (though Sunday Schools were chiefly initiated in the late 18th century by various bodies, and one clearly existed before this Dame's School, but probably not long before).

Lady Anne had left £50 a year to endow 'a preaching ministry at Balsall' and Lady Katherine specified 'a minister to read the Scriptures twice a day and instruct the almswomen for the good of their souls'; he was also 'to teach twenty of the poorest boys in Balsall constantly until they were fit to be apprenticed', and to take nothing from their parents, at a salary of £20 a year. As will shortly appear from the regulations laid down by the Governors for the School, this was no sinecure, and an assistant master was appointed in 1784 'to help with teaching the boys'. He was allowed a house, the west wing of the Court, which still has the name 'School House' on its door; this was the wing, corresponding to the Matron's house, which was

57 Dame's School, Haseley, on the Birmingham to Warwick road, five miles north of Warwick. Perhaps typical of the humble cottages used as schools at the turn of the century. The front door, left of the large window, is said to have been bricked up because a tramp walked in and stole a ham.

originally built 13 years before to house especially frail almswomen who needed particular care.[4]

The school rules are spelt out more explicitly in an undated memorandum which must post-date 1784 since it refers to the Assistant Master:

> It is ordered by the Governors that the following regulations shall be strictly observed in the school at Balsall Temple
>
> - That there shall be fixt holidays in the School and no others, that is, 2 weeks at Easter, three weeks in August and 3 weeks at Christmas
>
> - That the parents of the children may take them home in harvest time and keep them longer than the stated holidays if they think proper, but this is at the option of the parents and not of the Assistant Master
>
> - That the Assistant Master shall on no account omit his attendance in the School on Saturdays and that the boys are to attend in School on that day, and likewise at Church on Sundays
>
> - That no entrance money is to be given to the Assistant Master.[5]

Whether the rule about attendance on Sundays refers to a Sunday School is not clear. But what does emerge from this entry is that the Assistant Master had been taking the law into his own hands, awarding longer summer holidays, failing to appear on Saturdays, and taking entrance fees from the parents of the boys!

Apprenticeship

Under Queen Elizabeth, the Statute of Artificers of 1563, substituting a national policy for the local operations of the trade gilds, laid it down that every craftsman should learn his craft under a master who was responsible for him. It was a very practical answer to the ever-present problems of technical education and the difficult 'after-school age', a measure of social as well as economic control.[6]

Amongst the surviving apprenticeship indentures for Balsall, only one relates to an early pupil of the school: Richard Peyton (spelt in the indenture *Peaton*, but undoubtedly the same boy). He is described as 'a poore child of Balsall' and is apprenticed on 8 November 1683 to William Harborne of Balsall, yeoman, for seven years. A premium of 40s. is to be paid by the Overseers of the Poor to Harborne. The terms of the apprenticeship, standard for all apprentices (boys or girls) at this time, though later much modified, are worth quoting for the insight they give into the kind of life an apprentice might expect:

> He is to keep his master's [trade] secrets well and faithfully and his commandments—he shall do no furnicacion in the house of his said master—Taverns nor alehouses he shall not haunt except it be about his master's business—At the cards, dice or any unlawfull games he shall not play—matrimonie with any woman he shall not contract. Thomas Harborne promises to teach Richard in the way of husbandry, finding him good wholesome and sufficient meat, drink, apparel, lodging, washing, fire … and at the end of the said time to find him 2 whole suits of apparrell, one fit for holy days, the other for working days and 2s 6d for his salary or wages.[7]

Chapter 16

Digression
A Clandestine Marriage in the Old Hall

On 31 March 1670 a solemn gathering met in Meriden Church. Present were the vicars of Hampton in Arden, Packington, Meriden, the curate of Wroxall, Simon Morton a public notary, and many others. These constituted an ecclesiastical court. Its purpose was twofold: to inquire into the validity of a will, and the legality of a marriage contracted without banns or witnesses.

CHARLES HOLBECH, lawyer, presented the evidence on behalf of ANN EVETTS, widow of JOHN EVETTS, deceased son of CHRISTOPHER EVETTS of Temple Balsall. John was the executor and residuary legatee named in Christopher's will.[1]

Calling into question the legality of the marriage to Ann Evetts were LAURENCE EVETTS and FRANCIS EVETTS, younger brothers of John.

Holbech called a number of witnesses, who were sworn and made their depositions on this momentous day. All were asked how long they had known Christopher Evetts, John and Ann, and Laurence and Francis Evetts.

RICHARD PRETTY, vicar of Hampton-in-Arden, aged 59, stated that he asked Ann, after the death of her husband John, to bring in the will of Christopher, her father-in-law, to whom John was named as executor, on 30 January 1670. He testified that Christopher was always very rational and sensible, and that when he made his will in August 1667, he was *compos mentis*. Because John had not proved his father's will before his own death (Christopher died some time before 26 October 1669,[2] John the following Christmas), Ann was given letters of administration as regards the will and goods of Christopher Evetts. He (Richard Pretty) said that before John's death, on 8 July 1669, he had questioned John about a clandestine marriage in the Temple Hall at Balsall (i.e. The Old Hall). John said that Mr. Hunt, curate of Barston, had married them. Mr. Hunt on being questioned, admitted marrying John Evetts and Ann Gardner, and asked for forbearance. He said they lived together, and John called Ann his wife and she used to call him her husband. She had the power and privilege of a wife in the family, and all regarded her as his wife.

SAMUEL HUNT, curate of Barston, aged 34, testified as to Christopher's soundness of mind. He then stated that about 15 April 1669, John Evetts came to see him at Barston, confessed that he had got Ann Gardner, his servant, with child, and asked for advice. Samuel advised him to marry her. The following day he, Samuel, came to Temple Balsall and in the Temple parlour celebrated marriage. There were no others present. John said he was glad he had married her, and though he might have done better for himself, his wife would be careful of his business and they would not live above their means, whereas if he had made a higher match his wife would have looked for greater attendance. [Note: the incumbent at Barston had the cure of souls at Temple Balsall which was not endowed for a ministry until the wills of Lady Anne and Lady Katherine were proved].

ELIZABETH SMITH, spinster, aged about 52, servant in John Evetts' house, said that John Evetts and Ann Gardner got Mr. Hunt to come to Temple Balsall, and that they went into the great parlour, and Mr. Hunt produced a big book by which he married them. She suspected what was going on and got behind a broken wall and saw and heard what went on. [For the dilapidation of the Old Hall see Chapter 18.] John Evetts pulled a ring out of his pocket and put it on Ann's finger. She believed the marriage was consummated for next morning she wanted a key which Ann had and she went into the chamber and saw them in bed together.

THOMAS SOLEY of Balsall Street, aged 21, servant in the house of John Evetts, said that he saw the parties going towards the parlour, supposed that marriage was afoot and went out of the house through the stables and into a little shed with a window that looked into the parlour. He could not hear, but saw John holding Ann's hand and the minister with a great book. He said John called Ann wife until his death, and all reckoned them man and wife. [So though the marriage was clandestine, without banns, and seemingly without witnesses, it was nevertheless witnessed by two servants.]

GEORGE BRADNOCK of Berkswell testified that Ann had sole command of the house, under her husband. Also that when Ann was in labour, John doubting the competence of the midwife sent off a servant on a horse to find a better one.

THOMAS TAYLOR of Balsall deposed that he had been a servant to the grandfather and father of John Evetts and of John himself. He had been to their chamber for instructions about going to market and had seen John and Ann in bed together. If money needed to be spent on the house, John would say 'Ask Ann' and money from the sale of corn or cattle he was told to give to Ann.

NICHOLAS BOND of Cubbington, mason, employed on repairs to the chapel of Temple Balsall for a year, stayed all that time in John Evetts' house until John's death. He said Ann and John called each other wife and husband and lived lovingly together. When she was in labour John feared the midwife was not skilful and sent Nicholas to find a better one and later thanked him for his care for his wife.

ROBERT DORMAN of Barston was a near neighbour of John Evetts and often visited him. When he was dying Robert sat up with him, and Ann lay in another bed for John's comfort. She came and laid his arms over her. The next day he died.

LAURENCE FULFORD of Balsall, blacksmith, was one of the valuers of the goods of old Christopher Evetts and came to value the goods in the house; John Evetts being present would bid him not to set down such and such because they were not his father's goods but came to him as his wife's dowry. (For the inventory of Christopher's goods see Appendix IV, p.139.)

THOMAS EVETTS of Balsall, gentleman, brother of John, said he was told of the marriage which took place before the child was born. He said that Laurence and Francis [the disputing brothers] had been told and he believed they did not deny the marriage but only its lawfulness. He said that Ann Gardner, now Ann Evetts, was a servant in Christopher Evetts' house, not long before he died. She was so observant, dutiful and respectful to Christopher that when he heard that she was married to John he did not seem at all offended. [It is this Thomas who some four years later became the first Bailiff of the Lady Katherine Leveson Charity.]

OLIVER WEYHAM of Knowle deposed that at the end of sheepshearing in June he happened to be in John Evetts' company, and John wanting to see the progress of repairs to Temple Chapel [Lady Anne's restoration of the church was still ongoing in 1669], took him into his house and called for beer. He said 'My wife is not at home but I know where she has put her key' and then forthwith he took a knife and opened a box and took out the key and had the beer brought to him. While they were drinking Ann came in and went past them to the old man, Christopher Evetts. John called her back and introduced her as his wife.

MARGARET ALDEN, an old friend of Ann's though twice her age, said she believed Christopher liked the marriage and quoted him as saying 'I like very well of it and I think he could not have done better'. When the child was born he went in and picked it up and kissed it and prayed 'God bless it'. He said it was a pity it was a girl, but as it was, she was to be called Mary for his wife's name was Mary and he loved her very well. Margaret also stated that John had at least £100 as Ann's marriage portion.

MARTIN HOLBECH of Meriden, gentleman, lawyer and steward of the manor court of Temple Balsall, stated that he came to hold the court in April 1669 and met Ann there; she was very pregnant and he asked her if she was married. 'Not yet', she answered, 'but John has often promised marriage', and she thought he would be as good as his word. At the next three-weekly court he came again and asked her if she was married and she smiled and said, 'Yes, i'faith, I am married now'. Martin said that Thomas Evetts, John's brother, declared that 'She is too good for him and he could not have had a better or more useful girl to espouse'. He later held two more courts at Temple Balsall and the tenants came and Ann provided refreshments and governed the affairs of the house as mistress. Martin Holbech was invited to the christening, when Ann's brother Andrew was godfather, and the widows of Christopher Evetts and of Barlow Evetts, John's brother, were godmothers.

ANDREW GARDNER, aged 40, yeoman, brother of Ann Gardner, said he often visited John and Ann at Temple Balsall, and John treated him civilly and with much courtesy. At Christmas 1669 when John fell ill, he sent for Andrew and asked him to stay with him. Andrew held John's head, and John said 'Poore brother, I shall quite tyer you out'. Andrew then brought Ann in for she had been resting in another room. She knelt and put John's arms round her and he died shortly afterwards in her arms.

* * *

Ann Evetts was admitted as an almswoman to Temple Balsall Hospital on 12 February 1718 when Ann (Gardner) Evetts would be about 69 years old.[3] In 1727 Ann Evetts died, described as a widow, of the Lady Katherine Leveson Hospital.[4] In her will, after some small bequests, she left the residue of her estate to her daughter Mary, her executrix. This must surely be the widow of John Evetts, but by what stages she came to be admitted as an almswoman is not clear.

Comment

The original Ms of the above proceedings (A8/1670) is preserved in Lambeth Palace Library, a document from the court of Arches; this is a court of appeal belonging to the Archbishop of Canterbury, which determines appeals from inferior ecclesiastical courts. The action brought by the two Evetts brothers, Laurence and Francis, disputing Christopher's competence to make a will, and the legality of John's marriage to Ann, seems to be lost, but it is not difficult from the defence's evidence to deduce what the charges must have been in the case of the marriage: that Ann was a poor servant of low degree who had trapped the eldest son into marriage, and that she was unfit to take on the responsibilities of mistress of the household.

The defence consisted of evidence that Ann had not come penniless to the marriage (witness the household goods mentioned by Laurence Fulford, and the £100 'dowry' by Margaret Alden); that her brother Andrew was of yeoman status like John's father Christopher, and accepted socially by John Evetts; that Ann was competent as mistress of the household, from various sources. It is worth noting that the step from yeoman to gentleman is a small one, perhaps assisted by notable prosperity; at least two of Christopher's sons, Thomas the bailiff and Francis, were accounted a gentleman.[5]

The seriousness with which illegitimate birth was viewed can be seen from an instance at Clayworth (Nottinghamshire) where in April 1679 Ralph Meers and Ann Fenton were refused communion by the Rector as they were reputed to be living together but not married. Ann Fenton's first baby was christened on 10 June, by which time the couple had married, presumably outside the village.[6]

Chapter 17

Major Rebuilding at the Court

The Governors' Order Books are full of much interesting detail, but on some of the major decisions they are surprisingly laconic or even silent. Thus in 1708 it appears that 'more building is to be added to the hospital for the reception of poor women as the Governors judge it convenient to be done', without any indication of how this is to be carried out.[1] Three years later we find in the Register of Dames[2] that Hannah Arch and Christian Loom have been admitted into 'the new apartments' on 29 September, and the next year Susannah Fulford, Anne Clever and Mary Titmus were admitted into 'the new buildings'; it is now established that there are 25 women instead of the original 20 specified by Lady Katherine,[3] but how this extra accommodation was added is a matter for conjecture.

An extra two old women were somehow accommodated in 1720,[4] and the following year the Governors began considering how they might make additional building to the Hospital. They decided to ask Mr. Alderman Smith for assistance in the project. This was Francis Smith, Alderman of Warwick borough, architect and builder, who rebuilt the Court House at Warwick, and was surveyor of Warwick Castle from 1720 to 1735. He was responsible for many buildings in the town, as well as Stoneleigh Abbey and Umberslade Hall.[5]

It is not until 1725 that the next information emerges, and it is startling enough. It is resolved by the Governors 'that Francis Smith *do take down and substantially rebuild the other side of the hospital* on or before 1st November 1726 in such a manner as he has already built except as to the Master's Lodge where he is to lay a new floor and *make a cellar* and proper partitions for £500'.[6]

It is reasonable to suppose that Smith followed the first design of the buildings (for which we have Hurlbutt's specifications, as has been said), for much of the detail which still survives today can be seen to tally, notably the central pediments with their medallions, the 'framing' of the windows and doorways with stone, and the single doors to serve two apartments. Thus the new buildings would agree well with the Master's House which continued in its original design for another hundred years. Presumably the Dames had to share rooms with their neighbours across the Court during the re-buildings.

58   The south wings of the Court. Two Dames wearing regulation shawls and bonnets visit the School-house (west) wing on the Breadwalk. The Dames originally collected their bread allowance from the Old Hall, hence the name of the path. In 1902 the weekly allowance was reduced from 8 lbs to 6 lbs. (The east wing, Matron's House, can be seen on the right.) (Warwick CRO CR 1540/2, pp.120, 137.) The rule about wearing uniform was abolished about 1960.

It can be seen from the drawing (Fig.34) that the two ranges of almshouses were brought up to the height of the Master's house. The original dwellings must have been inconveniently low, and the additional height provided apartments upstairs rather than merely bedrooms for the ground-floor units (bedrooms which must have been extremely cramped for headroom, and largely within the roof space). The full width (19 feet between the main walls) was maintained, and the ground-floor apartments, with their more commodious height, could provide bedrooms on the flat as well as living-rooms. Building over the old boys' school-room, and the corresponding school-master's house on the west of the Master's house, to achieve a level height all round the Court, provided still more accommodation. In 1727 it was confirmed that the number of poor women was thirty.[7]

The south wings of the Court
It was almost fifty years before the next development in the Court. It was reported to the Governors in 1771 that 'one old woman was so old and infirm that she is in danger of setting fire to herself and the hospital, and others are likely to be reduced to the same state'. They resolved that additional building should be made for the reception of such women, and also for a matron so that they might be properly attended to. Plans were to be prepared for their next meeting.[8] This was the origin of the two

cross-wings built on to the south ends of the existing ranges of building. The east wing became the Matron's house (see above, Chapter 14) and remains so to this day; the west wing, originally designed for the most infirm Dames, later became the assist-ant schoolmaster's house (and has the name *School House* on its front door at present, though with the building of the modern school the staff situation and their accom-modation were all changed).[9]

It was not until the rebuilding of the Master's house in the next century that there was any further change in the general aspect of the Court.

Chapter 18

The Old Hall Ruinous and Temple House Built

In 1736 the Governors' attention was drawn to the ruinous state of the buildings at the Old Hall, and to the fact that many desirable conveniences were lacking, which could be supplied out of the material from the most dilapidated structures. They resolved to make a survey.[1]

The Old Hall had been the residence of the Evetts family since Christopher Evetts, a very prosperous yeoman, had taken a lease of Temple House Farm, the home farm of the long-gone Templars, in 1660.[2] His son, Thomas, was entrusted by Lady Katherine with the supervision of the estate as her bailiff, together with the day-to-day running of the Hospital. She obviously esteemed him highly, and styled him

59   Temple House: built for the bailiff of the Temple Balsall estate, and completed in 1740.

'gentleman' in her will, the first step up the social ladder for this well-to-do family. Further, she nominated him as a Governor of the Charity, on a par with the other 11 Trustees, who included the son of Lord Leigh and Sir William Bromley of Baginton.

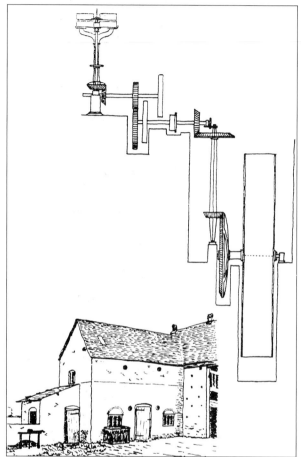

The office of Bailiff became an hereditary one, and the first five holders came from the Evetts family, from father to son in unbroken succession. But when in 1765 the post became vacant on the death of Thomas Evetts, his son, Thomas, was only four years old and his mother, Ann, widow of Thomas, was appointed, and served as 'our bailiff, Mrs Evetts' until 1776.[3] Thus, the first 100 years of this office was covered by the Evetts family. Tradition has always had a strong hold at Balsall.

It was the third Evetts Bailiff, the second Thomas, who had started to complain about the state of the Old Hall. In 1735 he began preparing for his retirement by assigning the lease of Temple House Farm to his recently married son, Barlow.[4] The next year, the architect, Mr. Francis Smith, who, 10 years before, had been responsible for rebuilding the Hospital, was asked by the Governors to prepare an estimate for repairing or rebuilding the Old Hall.

60 One hundred years on: Temple House farm wheel. In November 1851, Mr. Couchman, the Bailiff, asked the Governors to agree to the installation of a farm wheel at Temple House, and this was carried out by Robert Summers in 1852 at a cost of £610 17s. The waterwheel operated a single pair of stones to produce animal feeds as well as driving machinery in adjacent farms. The full pool drove the wheel for half a day. (Warwick CRO CR 1540/1, pp. 196, 197.) The wheel was dismantled in March 1983 and taken to Avoncroft Open-Air Museum. The plan of the farm wheel and sketch of the building housing it is from *Warwickshire Watermills*, by D.T.N. Booth, published by Midland Wind and Watermills Group, 1978.

61 View of Temple House from the east. The head of water to drive the wheel is shown in the foreground.

The medieval hall-section of the building, with the later parlour and chamber over, were to be preserved. This resolution was repeated the following year, with 'next spring' as the target date.[5]

But the plan for making the Old Hall fit for the new bailiff was suddenly abandoned and the Governors resolved to ask for plans for erecting 'a mansion house' for their next meeting which was to be as early in spring as convenient.[6] Events moved fast, for on 20 September 1739 they were deciding on the 'floor of the Hall of the house *late erected* at Temple Balsall'. As it stands today, it can be seen as a spacious mansion, comprising a cellar, pantry, garrets for the servants, a great parlour, various 'chambers and other rooms'. Mr Barlow Evetts, the bailiff, was to go and reside there with his family as soon as the house was fit to be inhabited, and all the old house he then inhabited (the Old Hall) was to be pulled down except the actual [medieval] hall and adjoining parlour. The old materials produced by the demolition were to be used towards erecting a house of office for the new dwelling.[7]

The finishing touches to the new house proceeded at a more leisurely pace,

62 Farm wheel. (Photo: *Coventry Evening Telegraph*, by permission.)

for in 1740 the Governors urged that the house was to be finished and made habitable without further loss of time.[8] Still lacking the following year were a dovehouse, a 'necessary house', pigsty and some walling, the finishing of the parlour and six window seats.[9]

There, Barlow Evetts and his wife Sarah settled in and added another nine to their existing three children. All were baptised at St Mary's church, Temple Balsall, by the minister of the time, and nine of the twelve survived beyond childhood.[10]

The Excavation of the Cellar

An excavation carried out in 1981 showed that on their departure from the Old Hall, the Evetts jettisoned a large quantity of household pottery and glass.[11] The survey of Balsall which was carried out by Henry VIII's Commissioners had noted a buttery with a cellar underneath, adjoining the Old Hall.[12] The buttery had no doubt been demolished in the tidying-up operations after 1736. But in 1981 the lawn on the south side of the building had a somewhat concave outline, which prompted the question whether it might conceal the cellar.

This proved to be the case, and the excavation revealed that the de-roofed cellar had been used as a dumping ground for unwanted pottery and glass. The Evetts presumably wanted more elegant and up-to-date wares to complement their fine new house. The finds included a number of whole vessels and others evidently broken on impact for they were capable of being almost entirely reassembled. Some bore dates or close dating marks, for example a large mug or 'pottle' with the incised date 1700 on its side, several beer mugs with the Queen Anne excise seal (1702-1714), a slipware dish with the stylised embossed 'portrait' of George I (with the initials GR and crown, 1714-1727), and a slipware dish decorated with the outline of a bird and the date 1728.

There were many wine bottles, whole or broken, and the study of these is sufficiently established for their range to be dated roughly from 1650 to 1740. The undated pottery is broadly assignable to periods from 1670 to 1740; it included blackwares (1600s to 1700), English delftware (c.1680 to 1740), manganese-mottled wares (1700s to c.1730), stonewares (1700s to c.1720), white-dipped stonewares (1710 to c.1750), Ralph Shaw's Patent-type wares (1740s) and tobacco pipes of the same general period, all of which were agreeable to the supposition that the Evetts had thrown them out on their departure for a more elevated life-style. It is not possible to do more than hint at the large quantity of material crammed into the cellar.[13]

The Old Hall was, and is, isolated—several minutes' walk from the almshouses— apart from its neighbour Temple House. It is fairly certain, then, that the collection of material came from one family (although some later material was obviously thrown in after the abandonment of the cellar, a fairly detailed map of 1759 shows no trace of an open cellar in front of the Old Hall).[14]

63 White delftware, London, late 17th century to 1750. Ointment/drug pots, basin and chamberpot; some tinged blue/grey.

64 Tea bowl, blue and white, probably London delftware, 7cm diameter.

65 High quality blackware, probably from Burslem.

66 Pipkin, yellow glaze on cream fabric, probably Ticknall ware.

67 English delftware bowl, London, 1700.

68 Manganese-mottled cups, Staffordshire, 1700-1715. The most numerous pots are in this ware, including cooking pots, mugs and chamberpots.

 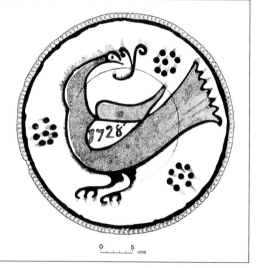

69 Two decorated dishes: cream fabric, lead-glazed; dark red slip for the outlines, mixed with cream slip for the slightly paler parts of the designs. Staffordshire; one dated 1728.

70 Combed and feathered slipware dish: brown slip (clay mixed with water to a painting consistency) covers the whole pot. This is then fired and covered with a cream slip which is combed with a zig-zag motion to reveal the brown coat underneath with a 'feathering' effect.

The Finds

The pottery is very variable in quality, ranging from very coarse low-grade vessels (some surely trade 'seconds' or rejects, probably survivals from older generations' crocks), to the highly finished and doubtless expensive Ralph Shaw's Patent-type wares. The particularly large quantity of brown manganese-mottled wares suggests that this was the family's staple everyday crockery, superseding the blackware of the early 18th century, and itself being ousted for better occasions by the stoneware. The small amount of white stoneware probably indicates that this was their latest acquisition, and that the specimens found were genuine breakages rather than unwanted discards. The total lack of English porcelain, together with the other evidence, serves to confirm the terminal date of the collection of finds.

The large number of whole or broken glass medicine phials, and a similar profusion of English delftware ointment pots suggests that the bailiff's house served as a pharmacy for the Dames and that their medicine was often doled out here as well as their bread allowance. The collection of remains as a whole bespeaks a generally modest life-style which may be compared with the remains of another household of a similar date-range (1650-1730). The cesspit of a Nottingham family excavated in 1973[15] yielded items such as Chinese porcelain, *decorated* ointment pots and a much greater range of Venetian-style glass table ware, all testifying to a more sophisticated way of life than that of the Evetts. Yet they had their wine glasses, some possibly Venetian, made for

71 Brown stoneware mug, dated 1700, height 20.4cm. The incised pattern is the earliest yet found; WR excise mark; Nottingham or Crich.

72 Selection of wine bottles found.

74 Two Piermont Water bottle seals. This spa water was exported from Germany in great quantities in the mid-18th century. Probably the water from the Old Hall well, situated below the cemetery, was already suspect.

73 Small selection of the many medicine phials, whole and fragmentary, excavated. Doubtless they once held doses for sick almswomen. 'Mr Bree of Solihull to attend and find medicines for the old women for 5 gns a year. If he decline, some other apothecary to be found' (Warwick CRO CR 1342/1 [1776]).

75 Wine bottle seal with initials 'TE' for Thomas Evett, one of the three Thomases occupying the Old Hall as bailiff. Gentlemen sent their own bottles, distinguishable by their seals, to be filled by their wine merchant straight from the barrel.

76 Tea break in the Old Hall—a rainy day on the dig.

the English market, and wine in abundance judging by the very large quantity of wine bottles, with evidence of spa water imported from Germany (Piermont Water), which was doubtless drunk in preference to the local well water. A bird feeder indicates the presence of caged birds, and several dishes were pierced for hanging as ornaments. A homely note is struck by the blackening on the sides of various mugs and cups, pushed up against the embers to warm up. An elegant copper-alloy riding spur perhaps matches the aspirations of this family rising in the world.

Where did the pots come from?

The Midland clays gave rise to many potteries from the middle ages onwards. Two were within striking distance of Temple Balsall—Wednesbury to the north-west of Birmingham, and Nuneaton to the north-east. Some Wednesbury blackwares have been excavated, but the trumpet-shaped cups and jugs have no parallels among the Balsall pots. Nuneaton produced many fine pots in the middle ages, but the best clays had been worked out by the 17th century, and only coarse-ware, often of poor quality, was then being produced. Nuneaton, then, may have been the source of the large red earthenware pancheons or bread-bowls found in the excavation.

At Ticknall, 12 kilometres south of Derby, there was a thriving industry in the 17th century, declining towards the end but persisting into the early years of the 18th century; the potters aggressively marketed their wares, travelling considerable distances and under-cutting local potters. It is likely that the yellow wares, such as the pipkin, and the second-quality blackwares, came from Ticknall. Only two potteries are named in the probate inventories of goods of Balsall (and also Nuneaton) inhabitants—Ticknall and London. But the potteries of Staffordshire were fast becoming a powerful factor, and there is little doubt that the bulk of the very fine blackwares (cups and chamberpots), came from Burslem or nearby potteries; also the

77 Among the potsherds: the author and her late husband, Arthur, at the Old Hall 1981 dig.

78 Members of the Coventry & District Archaeological Society who took part in the 1981 excavation at the Old Hall. Left to right: Carol Jordan, Ann Grills, Brian Jordan (behind), Valerie Goode, John Haslam (behind), David Warren, Maurice Kite, Peter Mather (behind), Dr. Arthur Gooder, Alan Burnett (behind), Eileen Gooder, Stella Graham (behind), Sheila Mather, Geoffrey Hawkins, Alan Birch (behind), Mike Manley, Ray Wallwork, Zena Wallwork (behind). The position and dimensions of the cellar, outlined in paving slabs, can be seen in front of the group.

mottled brown manganese ware (cups, jugs and chamber-pots) which were so numerous as to suggest that these had superseded the blackwares as the staple day-to-day crockery at the Old Hall.

By the late 17th century, Nottingham, as well as Stoke, was producing high quality brown stoneware, and the large mug dated 1700 may well have come from there, though Crich, 19 kilometres north of Derby, may just possibly have been the source.

Delftware, in the shape of the plain white ointment pots, and some decorated bowls and chamberpots, could have come from two areas—Bristol and London. As London, with Ticknall, was the only ware mentioned by name in the inventories, it is possible that London delftware predominated.

79 Ralph Shaw Patent-type mug.

Perhaps the most highly accomplished and sophisticated wares found in the excavation were the small number of Ralph Shaw Patent-type mugs. These are delicately thin, milky white inside and dark chocolate-brown outside, decorated with bands of grey/white grits. They must have come from Stoke.

Although no closely similar examples have been found to the two large bird plates, they have been ascribed to the Stoke potteries without hesitation by Dr. Henry Sandon.[16]

It is interesting to note that the finds included several German mugs, and a fine jug, all of a very thick, hard, durable pot, decorated with cobalt-blue motifs. They are all from Westerwald, an area north-east of Frankfurt.

Postscript   A similar cache of pottery and glass from an inn, of slightly earlier date, 1660-1700, was excavated in Guildford in May 1991. Reported in Surrey Archaeological Society Bulletin No.270 (November 1992).

Chapter 19

A New House for the Master

In 1834, just over a hundred years after the rebuilding of the almshouses, the Master's house was in obvious disrepair. Mr. Boultbee, a new Governor, was asked to order what repairs he thought necessary to Mr. Short's house and stables. Evidently he took a poor view of the state of the house, for the same year the Governors decided that a formal survey be made.[1]

The following January it was clear that the surveyor had produced a very serious report. The Master's house was declared to be in such a ruinous state that it was not fit to be repaired. Mr. Smith, the architect, of Leamington, was to be asked to prepare plans and give a close estimate for an entire re-build. As part of the bargain, he was to make apartments for three extra almswomen and a nurse above the old boys' schoolroom (where there was unused space since the roof of the schoolroom was raised to match the raising of the roof of the almshouses on that side in 1725).[2]

In August that year, Charles S. Smith produced plans and an estimate of 'not over £3,000' for the work, and 'he was to be responsible for painting, for the chimney pieces, firegrates, and the bells'. He was to be paid £150 for his plans, £15 a week during the building, and £500 for materials plus £3,000 between then and next Christmas. The Reverend Mr. Short was to have £100 to rent a house and defray his expenses whilst the new one was being built. The following January (1836) the Governors instructed their broker to sell enough of their three per cent Consols to provide the money as needed for the building. As the work was proceeding, they told Mr. Couchman, their bailiff, to advance money to Mr. Smith to make up what he had already received to £3,000, between then and 'Christmas next', presumably Christmas 1836, provided that the work he had contracted to do was properly completed before that time.[3]

In March 1837 Smith reported that the work on the house and the apartments was completed and they were fit for occupation. He presented his account of the expenses incurred, amounting to £4,080 12s. 7d. On comparing this with the 'close estimate' agreed in August 1835, it was clear that the cost exceeded the estimate by over £930. Not surprisingly the Governors did not feel authorised to advance money

80 The Court: Master's House and Hospital, 1990. (The poor quality of this reproduction is due to the unavailability of the original photograph.)

in addition to the £2,651 already paid to him on account until it was agreed by a full meeting (there were only four present at this meeting). A competent person was to be employed to survey the buildings to see how far Smith's account was a fair one, and a copy of their resolutions was to be sent at once to all Governors for their opinion. Accordingly, Joseph Plevin of Birmingham was asked to inspect the work and he reported that the new house, together with the additions over the schoolroom, were worth £3,646 (that is, over £400 less than Smith was claiming).[4]

The Governors evidently now stalled, for it is not until 1839 that more is heard from the architect, when he claimed £150 for his work on Mr. Short's house. The Governors, mindful that he had not properly fulfilled his engagement with them, but had left the building in an unfinished state, which had cost them an unexpected £100, decided to give Smith £50 (the bell was, in fact, not installed until 1842).[5]

Time passed until August 1841 when Smith again asked for £150 which he claimed as 'Architect in Building', superintending the erection of the Master's house. The Governors ordered their Bailiff to offer him £100 'without prejudice', and that seems to have been the end of the matter.[6]

It must be a matter of regret that the original Master's house, with its elegant south elevation harmonising so well with the almshouses, was not kept in sufficient repair to prolong its life to the present day.

Chapter 20

Schooling: Small Beginnings

Bedlam's End

From the middle of the 19th century, public attention was increasingly focused on the question of education for all. The Church was often the prime mover, as was the case at Bedlam's End.

Bedlam's End is the most southerly outpost of the manor of Balsall, abutting the turnpike road from Birmingham to Warwick (now A4711). Here, it appears, the educational initiative was taken, not by the Governors of the Lady Katherine Leveson Charity, but by the Reverend A. Morris, vicar of Hampton in Arden, in which parish Balsall lay until it was upgraded into an ecclesiastical parish in its own right in 1863.

In 1841 Mr. Morris applied to the Governors for a subscription towards 'purchasing a room' at Bedlam's End with a view to having it licensed as a chapel, and its being used as a schoolroom. The Governors resolved to subscribe £200 on condition that the 'building' was vested in five trustees, two of them Governors. Moreover, at an extra-ordinary meeting in October that year, they (though chiefly preoccupied with appointing a new schoolmaster and setting up a girls' school at Balsall) decided to pay the schoolmistress at Bedlam's End threepence a week for every child (presumably boy or girl) attending by permission of one Governor and the Master of the Hospital. That the little school was making a promising start is clear from the Governors' decision the next year to pay the schoolmistress five shillings a week so long as the children belonging to Balsall did not fall below fifteen, and that she be required to take all children recommended by the Master of the Hospital.[1] By inference, children were also coming from areas outside Balsall manor. This may possibly have been on the site of the original *'Tom O'Bedlam' Inn* (the more modern version of this was built alongside the old one before the latter was demolished).

The promising start turned into a roaring success, for by January 1844 there were almost fifty children attending the school. The Governors resolved that the schoolmistress's 'salary' should be increased by one shilling and sixpence a week 'until some arrangement is made about the Schoolroom', presumably to deal with overcrowding. They had received another letter from Mr. Morris two months earlier, proposing that

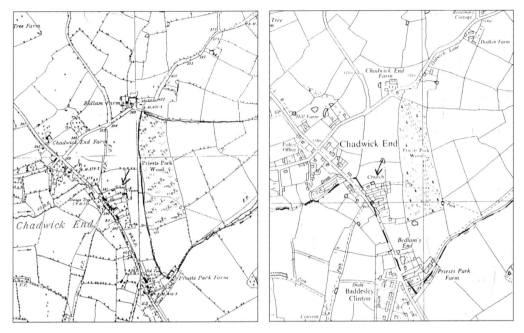

81   Chadwick End. The 1886 O.S. 6-inch map shows the school (© Crown copyright, MC99/351); the 1986 map, 10:10,000 metric shows the church (reproduced from the 1886 Ordnance Survey map).

they should take 'the house and chapel' at Bedlam's End at the sum he had agreed to pay for them, namely £498, that the sum of £200 now in his hands (which the Governors had supplied three years before), deducting two years' interest from the purchase money, should form a fund towards the expenses connected with the performance of divine service, or for the erection of a permanent chapel of ease, to which a district would be assigned. His letter continued to the effect that the school now had nearly fifty children; the house would form a desirable residence for a schoolmistress, and he himself would be glad to pay an annual rent of £10 or £12 for the use of two of the rooms for a curate. They ordered that Mr. Whateley, their solicitor, should write to Mr. Morris, saying that they would take the purchase (of the house) off his hands, and that they undertake to continue the chapel as a school and permit it to be used as a place of divine worship as long as Mr. Morris 'provided the duty'.[2]

At the normal August meeting of the Governors the same year, Mr. Whateley reported the result of his communication with Mr. Morris (which presumably was more or less a repetition of the burden of Mr. Morris's earlier letter), but after consideration they decided not to proceed with the negotiations, offering instead to give a site for a chapel of ease, and to contribute to the endowment of a fund if one could be raised to erect it.[3]

But when Mr. Morris wrote the next year asking for a site to build a chapel on, and for a contribution towards the cost of erecting it, the Governors decided to postpone the matter until there was a larger meeting, for there were only three present that day. It is evident, however, that a site was found nearby, at Chadwick End (see Fig.81) where a school/chapel was built. But by 1872 'the licensed building at Chadwick End, now used as a chapel' was out of repair, and a new dual-purpose one was erected in 1875, for 45 children. It was licensed for divine service every Sunday at 6.30 p.m. The average attendance was thirty-nine. The school was discontinued by 1900. The site of the building can be seen on the 1886 OS map, marked as a school. On the 1986 OS map (1:10,000 metric) the building is shown as a church, though by that date its useful life was over. For the rest of the building's short existence, when it was used solely as a church, see below under 'St Chad's Church'.[4]

The 'Bedlam Schoolmistress' continued to receive her 6s. 6d. a week from 1845 until at least 1870 and the Governors paid an annual £15 to the 'new school at Chadwick End', starting in 1875. The same year they resolved that Sarah Phillips, 'the late Infant Schoolmistress at Bedlam', should have an annual pension of £15 a year for life.[5] As in 1867 they had ordered that 'children should not remain at the Dame's School at Chadwick End beyond 8 years of age unless under special circumstances to be approved by the Master of the Hospital', it appears that the Bedlam and Chadwick End Dame's schools co-existed for a few years.[6]

In 1868 the Governors voted to allocate £10 a year for 'a proposed Dame's School at Balsall Street', and 'the Dame's School at Balsall Street will be of great use to young children who cannot come to the main schools at Temple Balsall'. The Governors tended to refer to primary or infant schools as Dame Schools. The named location is confusing, as there was no school in Balsall Street until the Balsall Street Council School was built in 1913, but Balsall Street was regarded as an area as well as a thoroughfare; for example, Thomas Wedge's map of Temple Balsall Manor (1779-80) names the area west of the street as 'Balsall Street Quarter'. There is no doubt that Holly Lane School was being referred to in this passage.[7]

An Early Core-Curriculum?

The present writer is old enough to have had a very brief experience of a village dame school in 1918-19. Some five or six of us were ushered into the sitting-room where the teacher sat with a small blackboard beside her. She rose and impressively wrote the word 'NOUN' on her blackboard, to the wild surmise of at least one five-and-a-half year-old. Memory fails after this fleeting snapshot, but evidently the lady was about to embark upon the mechanics of English grammar to pupils of tender years. How times have changed!

Balsall: a Schoolroom for Girls

At the same time that events were stirring at Bedlam's End, the Governors decided that something should be done about the girls at Temple Balsall. They resolved in

82   Annexe, still surviving, on the west end of School House. Perhaps the girls' school, pulled down in 1871, was behind the annexe in what is now the School House garden.

1841 to build a schoolroom for girls at the end of the schoolmaster's house, under the direction of Mr. Boultbee and Mr. Clive. This has been taken to mean the small annexe at the west end of School House, where the neo-Gothic windows fit the date very neatly. But when the new Boys' and Girls' School was built, the Governors ordered the Girls' School to be pulled down and in 1871 one Peach was paid: 'For taking down the Girls School and making the Boys School into the Prayer Room, with two sets of almshouses and taking down and rebuilding garden and Hospital walls £154 11s 4d'. Perhaps the Girls' School was an extension behind the annexe.[8]

Meantime the then schoolmaster, William Assinder, had become incapable through old age, and the Governors retired him on a pension of £30 a year on condition that he gave up his house. The Master of the Hospital, Mr. Short, was instructed to advertise in one London paper and in Aris' *Birmingham Gazette* for a schoolmaster and schoolmistress to teach boys and girls, on a joint salary of £80 a year with the use of the house. In October that year Mr. George Osborne and his wife were appointed to the joint position in lieu of William Assinder.[9]

The Reform Bill of 1832 set aside £20,000 a year for education, and by 1840 the machinery was in existence for making grants towards building premises for education—the applicants were to make sites permanently appropriated to education. This involved government inspection of the schools then established.[10] It is reasonable to assume that the Governors took advantage of the grant-aid towards the building of the girls' schoolroom, for in August 1851 an inspector, Mr. Smyth, reported to the Governors that on 3 February he had inspected both schools; he was much pleased with both of them, especially the girls who showed great proficiency and reflected great credit on the mistress. At the same meeting the Governors authorised George Osborne to engage an assistant for his wife as schoolmistress until Christmas because of her illness.[11]

A new development was the imposition of a fee of twopence a week on '*all but the labouring classes*' attending the schools. The money, the 'school pence', was to go to the schoolmaster and schoolmistress in addition to their salaries, which by then were £60 for the master, £40 for the mistress, an overall increase of £20 a year since the joint appointment at £80. (The Osbornes had perhaps retired by then and been replaced by two unmarried teachers.) Cloaks and bonnets were to be provided for the girls where necessary.[12] A later regulation suggests the existence of a marked class distinction, when 'girls paying 6d a week were to be allowed to wear their own bonnets and shawls'.[13]

A disquieting episode is reflected in an entry for 1862. Mr. Short, the Master of the Hospital, reported a complaint made by one James Harrison, through Mr. Kimbell, the medical attendant at the Hospital. He alleged that the illness and death of his daughter Eliza was the result of a severe caning from the schoolmistress (who was present at the meeting). Mr. William Floyd of Berkswell also attended, and made the same complaint. But 'it appeared from the statements of Mr Short and Mr Kimbell that the death of the child was caused by disease of the heart and other causes and could not be in the slightest degree attributed to the treatment she received from the schoolmistress'.[14]

Boys and Girls

A formal declaration of the rules for both schools was made the same year: they were to be open to all the children of the inhabitants of Balsall between the ages of five and 15, subject to the approval of Mr. Short and one of the Governors; they must come clean in person and dress on pain of 'forfeiting three tickets or some other punishment'. (It has not been possible to elucidate the ticket system.) Books and writing materials were to be provided by the parents, but might be purchased from the teachers at reduced prices. The schools were to open every morning with prayers, and anyone who was too late was to forfeit a ticket and be placed at the bottom of the class. The end of school each day was to close with prayers.[15]

Mr. Smyth, the Schools Inspector, visited Balsall again, in 1860 and 1861. He reported first that 'both schools were satisfactory, the Girls being especially well-conducted', then, at the second visit, that they were both 'very tolerable', 'the Girls efficiently conducted, the Boys not so satisfactory'. He judged that the Master needed assistance.[16]

83 Lady Katherine Leveson's School, Temple Balsall, built 1868, catering for both boys and girls.

Since there were no less than 70 boys aged between five and 15 on the register by this time (a daunting prospect within the confines of the Schoolroom) it is small wonder that they were less 'well-conducted' than the girls.[17] But the Log Book does not record such a high number of boys attending regularly; the number averaged only 51 for the past week on 27 July 1866. Attendance varied considerably according to the weather—on 18 October 1866 there were only 20 boys present 'owing to the weather', though 3 August that year saw as many as 66 attending. No doubt suitable clothing and footwear for bad weather were beyond the purses of many of the parents.[18] Assistance for the Master came in the form of a pupil teacher and in fact the girls' school was also to have one, the boy on a salary of £10 a year for his first year, the girl £8; these 'salaries' were to be increased by 50 shillings each year, and the pupil teachers were to be formally apprenticed.[19] But a more radical solution was called for, and the Governors began to plan for a new school for both boys and girls.

In 1866 they instructed their bailiff, Mr. Couchman, to get plans for a new school from Mr. Garner, architect, of Warwick. The present girls' school they planned to turn into a house for the schoolmistress (some extra accommodation being necessary since the days of the Osbornes who held the joint post and were housed together in School House). Tenders were invited.[20]

The Governors held a special meeting in July 1867 when it was reported that the lowest tender, £1,167 10s., from Jeffrey and Pritchard of Birmingham, having been accepted, building was already going forward. Always sensitive to appearances at Temple Balsall, they decided that Yardley Red tiles should be used for the roof instead of Broseley tiles. The plan to turn the girls' school into a house for the schoolmistress evidently fell through, for the next suggestion was to convert the former Matron's

84 The school: rear elevation, the Hospital perimeter wall on the left. It was clearly built as close as possible to the wall to maximise space in front of the school. (Photo: Derek Robinson.)

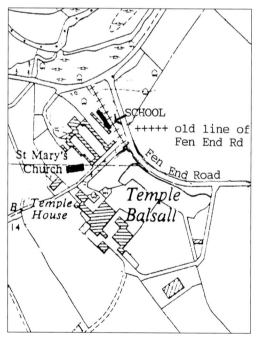

85 The school: diversion of Fen End Road to give a bigger playground.

house corresponding to the schoolmaster's house into a dwelling for the schoolmistress. This had earlier been used as accommodation for two almswomen. To compensate, two new almshouses were to be made over the boys' schoolroom; it is surprising that there was still room for these after the activities of the architect Charles Smith. The present girls' school was to be pulled down.[21]

It was reported in August 1870 that the school buildings were complete and the road diverted to give a larger playground for the children. This was Fen End Road, which originally ran immediately in front of the school, and was now moved to join the road to Knowle further east.[22]

The Role of the Master

By Lady Katherine's will, his role was to be multiple, primarily as vicar of the church, responsible for services and the spiritual welfare of the almswomen, then as Master of the Court with a general overview to ensure its orderly running, lastly as a teacher of the poor boys of the little school. The school-teaching had been delegated for some time when William Assinder was pensioned off in 1841, but he had, generally together with a governor, the decision about admissions to the school, and he made regular weekly or bi-weekly visits to the new school.[23] When the school was opened in 1868, the Governors laid it down that 'the course of instruction shall be under the direction of the Master of the Hospital', and they also declared that 'the school is quite of an elementary character'.[24]

86   Temple Balsall schoolchildren: probably between 1915 and 1918. (Temple Balsall Archive)

Later Schools in the Area – Holly Lane (Balsall Street) School

In 1871 the education department of the Privy Council (forerunner of the Board of Education) decided that an additional school for 60 children was needed in Holly Lane. The Governors were at first resistant, considering that there was enough provision already. They evidently had a change of heart, however, for the next year they voted an annual £20 to the 'Balsall Street Infant School', and later, a donation of £33 (half the building debt remaining on the school) and £30 p.a. (reduced to £25 p.a. subsequently) in support.

The Governors' resistance to the school and fears that it might detract from the Temple Balsall schools were to some extent justified, for in 1883, eight years after its opening, it was found that the Girls' School at Temple Balsall was not so well attended as before, 'the girls preferring to attend the mixed school at Balsall Street'.[25]

Extracts from the School Log Books give a vivid impression of schooling at Holly Lane. Children from the area had had to walk to Temple Balsall ('the Temple') for their schooling, two miles as the crow flies, but much further along the country lanes. The weather was a serious hazard for poor children, whose best protection was a sack over the shoulders.

As in the school at Temple Balsall, attendance was low because of the weather on many occasions—severe snow twice caused the school to be closed down (once when they were also out of coal). But there were pleasanter reasons for absence—the Coventry Fair in June 1877, and 'merry-making' at Berkswell the next year. Life was

87 Temple Balsall schoolchildren. (Temple Balsall Archive)

still close to the soil, when the children helped with hay-making, bean-setting and acorn-picking for the family pig.

The standards of health revealed by the school log books were alarmingly low: 'school closed, scarlet fever in the district' (12 July 1876); 'nearly all the children have troublesome coughs' (14 May 1877); 'several children sick with mumps' (29 October 1883); 'many absent with chicken-pox and whooping coughs' (20 April 1885); 'measles, diphtheria and consumption rife in Berkswell—at least three children dead' (15 February 1886); 'whooping cough epidemic, school closed two months' (7 June 1912); 'many in isolation hospital with scarlet fever' (October 1912). In March 1883 children from Berkswell (which seems to have been especially unhealthy) were excluded from the school 'because of fever'. (In the Act of Parliament of 1861 it was laid down that children from neighbouring parishes might be eligible for admission.)

In 1885 Her Majesty's Inspector reported that the school was overcrowded and an extra classroom would improve efficiency (the room was 25 feet by 17 feet, with a gallery for the infants and one outside lavatory, with which to seat 55 children). By 1890 there were 73 children on the books, and the Inspector was asking if the building might be enlarged. Still later (in 1907) he was commenting on the lack of space, dirt on the walls, floor in need of repair, and the infants in an 'old and very unsuitable gallery in a dark corner … it is quite impossible for them to receive suitable, or healthy training'. Not surprisingly there had been no less than 15 teachers in the 23 years of the school's life.

On 19 September 1913 this school was finally closed, its place being taken by the new Balsall Council School: 'Children on books 36, attendance 97.7%'.[26] The building was then used as the Church Hall for St Peter's Church, but was ultimately pulled down and rebuilt as the local Scouts/Guides' Headquarters.

Chapter 21

The Church (4)
George Gilbert Scott's Restoration: 1849

In the years since 1663, when Lady Anne Holbourne rescued the chapel, then in a ruinous state after the Reformation and the subsequent century of neglect, it had received only minimal attention. The question of a chapel-of-ease at Bedlam's End perhaps drew the Governors' attention to the mother church at Temple Balsall, for the same year, 1844, they resolved that the state of St Mary's should be inspected.[1] At their usual August meeting the following year, they instructed Mr. Couchman, their bailiff, to write to Messrs Scott and Moffat, architects, about necessary repairs to the church (variously called church or chapel until 1863 when it became the parish church).[2]

George Gilbert Scott had been a pupil of Sir Robert Smirke, who designed the British Museum, and restored York Minster (1811) among other projects. After his pupillage, Scott went into partnership with W.B. Moffat, and they built many public buildings 'of the work-house class'. Scott won an open competition to restore the church of St Nicholas, Hamburg, and his career took off. He was appointed architect for the cathedrals of Ely, Hereford, Lichfield, Salisbury and Ripon. He was knighted in 1872, but before his death in 1878 he had become notorious for excessive, over-confident restorations which robbed churches of character and individuality. In the last year of his life the Society for the Protection of Ancient Buildings was founded in hopes of counteracting his activities. The restoration of St Mary's is of some general importance as showing that Scott, in his early career at least, was in fact scrupulously sensitive to the age and character of the building. He recommended its 'perfect restoration to a condition worthy of so exquisite a specimen of ancient art ... [which must] have been

88 St Mary's Church, east end 1848. (Warwick CRO PV Tem. Chu. 4, from Brandon's *Parish Churches*, 1848.)

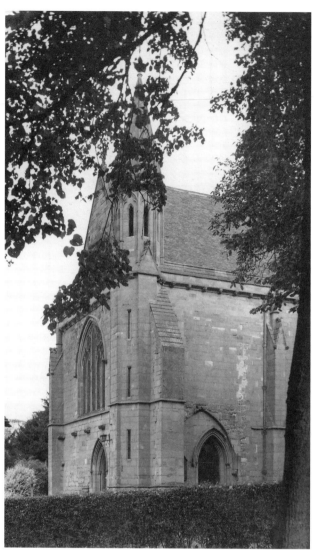

89 South view of Temple Balsall church, showing the remains of the former porch.

designed by one of the first artists of the day. [The restoration] would render it one of the most beautiful chapels (considering its simplicity and moderate dimensions) which are to be found in England.' His projected costs amounted to over £3,500![3]

In August 1846 Scott and Moffat were asked to show plans and give estimates for the restoration of the walls, roof and bell-turret of St Mary's. They lost no time, and next month Scott attended a special meeting of the Governors and reported on the insecure state of the south wall. He produced two sketches for the restoration of the roof. The Governors ordered that the foundations and drains on the north side should be repaired according to Scott's instructions provided that this cost no more than £100. Scott was asked to do working drawings of the new roof, and for the

90 One of a series of engravings made by H. Bowman and J.S. Crowther entitled *The Churches of the Middle Ages* (1857). The south elevation of St Mary's Church, Temple Balsall. (In a bound volume, Warwick CRO CR 2472, plate 4, by permission.)

restoration of the walls and the bell-turret. In November the same year Scott produced drawings for the new roof and was asked for specifications and estimates. In January 1847 they resolved that the restoration should go ahead under Scott's direction, and in August reviewed the question of timber for the new roof; some had been cut down on the estate, but there was not enough—more was to be bought in.[4]

By the following September, four builders had submitted tenders for restoring the church; that of Messrs Benjamin Broadbent and William Hawley of Leicester was the lowest (£1,300) and was accordingly accepted. Scott had now thought of some modification of his original proposals, most importantly the suggestion of strengthening the roof with a tie beam in the centre of the roof, but the Governors asked him to leave this out if it could be done with safety.[5]

91 Carved stone head found in the churchyard, probably from the church, appears to be medieval.

92 Interior of the Old Hall, *c.*1850, before it
was divided into the curate's and verger's cottages. It shows the furniture thrown out of the
church at the restoration—the old almswomen's
benches and the wooden pulpit, which from 1755
had a canopy over it to improve hearing (Warwick CRO CR 112/177/1). Also previously in the
church, Lady Katherine's hatchment and the
royal arms. Watercolour by Alan Everitt (1824-
82). (The Aylesford Collection, Birmingham
Central Reference Library, by permission.)

The work was evidently going well,
for in November 1848 Scott produced
plans for the interior of the church—a
vestry, 'interior fittings', and for re-laying
the floor with Staffordshire tiles, at a cost
of £700. The Governors sanctioned this.
The following April Scott produced plans
for a warm-air system which was to cost
£60 including necessary brickwork. Fired
with enthusiasm as the project neared its
end, the architect recommended painted
glass for the windows, but the Governors
could not afford this.[6]

At the Governors' usual August
meeting in 1850, it was decided to insure
the church for £1,000, and Scott was asked
to provide drawings for the pinnacles, and
state whether he thought the parapet
should be lowered. The pinnacles, of
course, are more than a decorative feature,
for they counteract the sideways thrust of
the roof which can easily damage the walls.
It was later decided that the pinnacles
should be executed in Kenilworth stone,

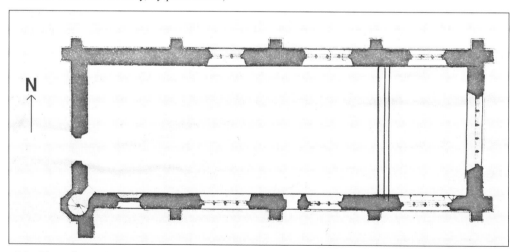

N
↑

93 Plan of Temple Balsall Church: note only three steps up to the altar. The floor must have sloped
up from the west door, as in Burton Dasset church. (From Brandon's *Parish Churches* [1848], photocopy Warwick CRO PV TEM. Chu. 6.)

and the three south windows painted green to exclude the sun. A harmonium was to be bought for use in the church.[7]

It is clear from Scott's surviving specifications that he proceeded with the utmost respect for the building and its fabric:

> The whole of the present roofing to be carefully taken off without injury to the walls, the old tiles to be cleaned and put in a place of safety for the purpose of being re-used ... the old timber to remain the property of the Trustees and to be re-used ... to such an extent as may be thought advisable ...

> All the decayed or defective Ashlar and Mouldings to be removed and good carefully introduced exactly agreeable to the original design, such portions whose features are not much damaged may be allowed to remain ...

> It is intended that all features which are not much mutilated ... be retained ...

> The internal stonework to be carefully cleaned of all whitewash and the natural clean surface of the stone exposed ... all the carvings which are obliterated to be restored but such as are but partially mutilated to remain so ...

> Generally, of all repairs, all the work to be done in the most substantial and careful manner with due regard to original form and substantiality ...[8]

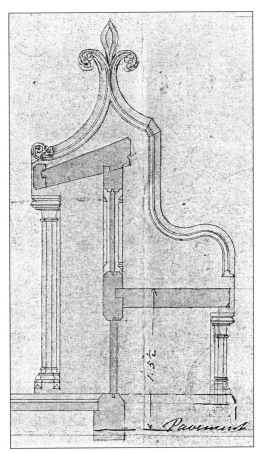

Nikolaus Pevsner laments the state of St Mary's: 'The sad thing is only that so much of it is by Sir George Gilbert Scott who restored *and largely rebuilt it* in 1849' [my italics].[9] The pulpit, sedilia and piscina are certainly all Scott's work, but otherwise it is clear from Scott's surviving papers that St Mary's today is a fair representation of Lady Anne Holbourne's church, tracery and all.

But Scott made three important changes to the structure of the church, two entirely justifiable. First, he restored the north and south walls to their original heights, for in Lady Anne's restoration the roof was taken down too low, sitting

94 Scott's working drawing of a pew (from Warwick CRO CR 1540/3/32), the subject of a violent quarrel between the Clerk of Works and the builder.

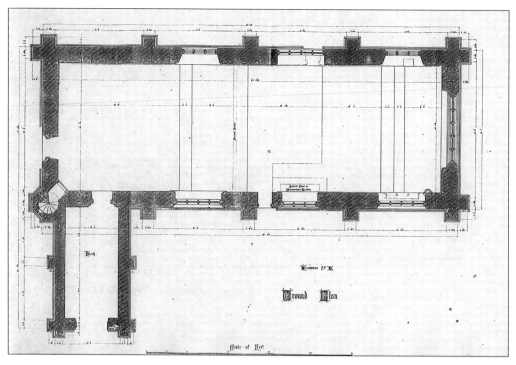

95   Ground plan of St Mary's from *The Churches of the Middle Ages* by H. Bowman and J.S. Crowther, vol.I (1857). The old rood screen was just east of the first two windows (from the west). (Information from G.G. Scott's notes.) Note: the former porch, as revealed by excavation, has been drawn as though still extant.

uncomfortably almost on top of the apex of the windows. Five courses of ashlar walling were needed to recover the original heights. Perhaps reasons of economy dictated the 17th-century decision. Secondly he re-designed the bell-turret, which in any case was in serious need of repair. Lady Anne's bell-tower, as seen in early water-colours (Figs.25, 29, 88) was heavy and obtrusive, in no way agreeing with the de-scription of Henry VIII's commissioners—'the steeple, a very little one …'. It is very unlikely that Scott ever saw this manuscript, but his instinct was clearly truer than the 17th-century architect's. (Henry Hewlett Raymond, a barrister of Grays Inn, researched the history of the chapel in 1857, but with the emphasis on its legal standing, the question of tithes, and the right of patronage as belonging to the manor. This re-search, undertaken after the restoration, was connected with the project of elevating the chapel into a parish church.)[10]

The third alteration was more controversial. The floor originally sloped to the three steps up to the sanctuary (see Fig.93, p.106) but Scott 'terraced' the floor with five more steps (one, then two double ones). This has the effect of making the more westerly pews seem sunken and out of touch with events at the altar and pulpit.

In a major work such as this there must have been many difficulties, frustrations, clashes of temperament. Charles Couchman, the Bailiff, refers to one such episode in a letter to Scott in December 1848.

> Mr Bell [clerk of works] and Mr Broadbent [builder] don't agree at all about the plan of making the seats; they have quarrelled violently and as far as I could understand they are equally blameable, so that I hope Mr Bell will find you at home on Monday morning that he may have your directions as to the greatest number of joinings that it will be safe to allow, that we may use up as much of the timber as possible.

Scott had been pressing rather persistently for some coloured glass in the church, and the Bailiff knows they cannot afford it. He concludes his letter: 'I am sorry to find that the coloured glass will cost us as much as £1 a foot—the Governors will scarcely be able to afford it'.[11]

96   G.G. Scott's pinnacles on St Mary's Church, photographed in 1996, showing decay. (Photo: Derek Robinson.)

Amongst the many papers relating to Scott's restoration of St Mary's is a plan of the floor of the church showing the memorial tombstones, presumably in preparation for the re-tiling. (Minton encaustic tiles of very high quality were used at a cost of £106 7s. 8d. They are still as good as new.)[12] In June 1981 members of the Birmingham and Midland Society for Genealogy and Heraldry made a plan of the existing tombstones.[13] Ignoring the wall-plaques, Scott's plan has 17 tombstones, and the 1981 plan has 19, presumably two being post-Scott. Their positions differ in the two plans, and it looks as though Scott 'tidied them up' in the re-tiling. The important difference in the two plans, however, is that Scott shows 11 stones under the sanctuary. These probably pre-date those in the body of the church, and may relate to persons of importance at the time of their death. For the names on the memorial inscriptions see Appendix V.

The East Window
It was over fifty years before G.G. Scott's earnest wish, that the east window of St Mary's should be filled with coloured glass, came to fruition. The existing glass must

97 The East Window with detail of the Annunciation from bottom of central light. (Photos: Pam Taylor, M.A.)

have been in a poor state, for in 1891 Messrs Hardman of Birmingham offered to glaze the window and the small window in the gable above with glass similar to that in the side windows, for £75. The Governors accepted the offer and the work was quickly completed.[14]

The idea of installing stained glass as a memorial to Queen Victoria's Jubilee was mooted in 1897, and public subscriptions were invited.[15] Several years passed, the Governors decided to employ Mr. Thomas Garner, architect, of Warwick (possibly the same who had designed the new school 30 years before), to produce a design, stipulating that the total cost should not exceed £400. Garner duly made a tentative draft, and several modifications were requested, including changing the figure of the Almighty to that of Christ. But by 1902 the uncomfortable fact emerged that the £400 took no account of carriage and fixing, to say nothing of the architect's fee of 10 per cent, and the Governors ruefully admitted that they had been 'unable to make further arrangements as to the East window for the present'.[16]

The records are unhelpful about the window. The Bailiff's Account Book, which would have recorded the payment to the designer and makers, is missing; no list of subscribers seems to have survived, and the Governors' Order Book now merely has the bald statement that a new design for the east window was requested.[17] As no other artist is mentioned, presumably the unfortunate Thomas Garner was required to rethink his design yet again. Amongst miscellaneous records in the Bailiff's deed box is a small postcard from Lord Aylesford dated 3 June 1905, approving the design of the armorial bearings (which now feature at the bottom of the east window glass)[18] so evidently the project was now moving again, and a church guide, written by the Rev. F.R. Fairbairn in 1926, states that the window was made by Messrs James Powell and Sons of London in 1907. In the Bailiff's Account Book, from July 1906, item 49 for the year beginning July 1907 reads 'Powell and Son examining East window—£2 2s 6d'. Presumably they were checking the installation of the window. Despite exhaustive searches, this is the only instance of the name Powell which has been found in original records. Presumably payment for the window was recorded in an earlier account now lost.[19] Fairbairn was vicar from 1902 till 1931, and in August 1907 asked permission to rearrange the east end of the church; the Governors postponed a decision but the following year allowed him to remove the retable from behind the altar and put a curtain in its place. This was presumably with reference to the new window. Further confirmation of the date 1907 appears on a Christmas card showing the detail of the Annunciation from the window, with the attribution 'Powell, 1907'.[20]

An undated statement issued by 'Holbeche and Son, Land Agents' lists the cost of the stained glass as £750 for the large window in the east end of the church, £50 for the small one (above), and £150 for the small circular one at the west end.[21]

James Powell and Sons (later Greyfriars Glass), founded in 1834, are still in existence, now specialising in vessel glass, bowls, goblets, vases and the like, of very high quality.[22] Their stained glass appears in churches in 21 counties and includes nine east windows, work in the Anglican Cathedral of Liverpool, and five Oxford college chapels. Christchurch Cathedral, Oxford, has two Powell windows, both designed by Burne-Jones.[23] John Hardman, now of Smethwick, continues to service the plain glass in St Mary's to the present day.[24]

98   Carved heads from the west end of St Mary's. (Photos: Alan & Elsie Birch.)

Carved Heads from the West End of St Mary's

These were seen by William Smith F.R.S.A. in 1829-30, that is before Gilbert Scott's restoration of the church in 1849. He describes 'a row of ten heads on a cornice or moulding at the west end ... of excellent workmanship'.[25] Two of these heads look as though they may be replacements made by Scott of especially weathered heads, but the four here photographed appear to be genuine medieval survivals.

It is certain that the heads on the south front are all Victorian, for Scott raised the height of the wall by five courses, and the 1804 drawing of the church shows no heads above the windows.

Chapter 22

The Church (5)
St Mary's becomes a Parish Church Now
Her Daughter Churches

On 12 March 1855, after 57 years in office, the Rev. John Short 'Master and Chaplain', died at Temple Balsall. The Governors met on the 24th, asserted their right of presenting a new chaplain, and expressed their wish that St Mary's should become a parish church and have an ecclesiastical district assigned to it. They ordered Mr. Whateley, their solicitor and Steward of the Courts, to apply to the patrons and incumbent of the church of Hampton in Arden, in whose parish Temple Balsall lay, to agree to their application to the Ecclesiastical Commissioners for a district to be assigned for, of course, it would be out of the parish of Hampton. They also asked that Hampton should contribute no less than £50 a year to the new incumbent, while they undertook to supply an adequate stipend in addition.[1]

But the Rev. A. Morris, vicar of Hampton, whose enterprising spirit we have met in Chapter 20, taking time by the forelock, had already, on 21 March, written to the Bishop of Worcester in whose diocese Hampton then lay, nominating the Rev. John Townsend, associate of King's College, London, 'to perform the office of curate in my chapel of Balsall in the parish of Hampton in Arden'; he promised to allow him £50 a year (Lady Anne Holbourne's bequest), and laid it down that he was to reside in a house in Chadwick End, two miles from the chapel.[2]

In April, Mr. Whateley was deputed to investigate the whole question of the rights of the vicar of Hampton as a charity involved with Temple Balsall and Lord Leycester's Hospital (through Lady Katherine's will), also the right of presentation to the chapel. The Governors did not think it necessary to delay for the results of these deliberations, but robustly ordered that the Rev. John Holbeche Short, son of the deceased vicar, be elected as the new chaplain, and then disposed of the chapel to him, a *fait accompli*, if ever there was one.[3]

The Bishop accepted the Governors' nomination, as it appeared that Mr. Morris had no claim to presentation whatsoever. Three Governors were then deputed to confer with the patrons and incumbent of Hampton on the question of forming the hamlet of Temple Balsall into a separate ecclesiastical district to be attached to the chapel.[4]

A year later, the Charity and Church Building Commissioners agreed that the hamlet should be formed into a district chapelry, but did not think it would justify raising the incumbent's salary.[5] The Governors' right of presentation was confirmed, and in December 1856 Mr. Morris withdrew his opposition to the forming of a district. The Governors decided to go ahead with their plan, and to appoint the Master

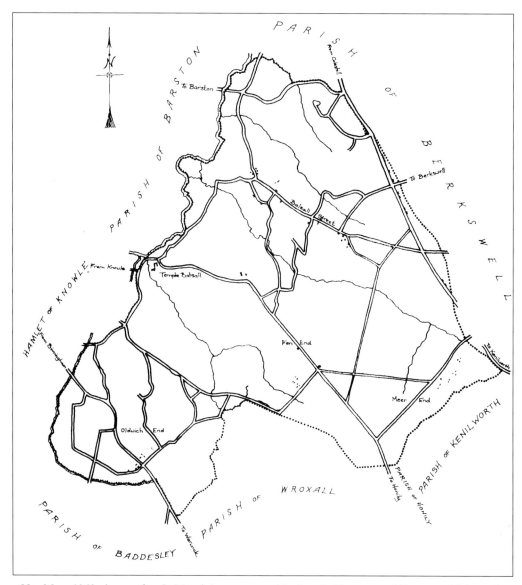

99   Map, 1963, drawn after St Mary's became a parish church. Note part of Barston which was in the old manor of Balsall here omitted as Barston had its own church. (Bailiff's chest of MSS)

of the Hospital as minister, with the understanding that he appoint a curate to assist him.[6]

In January 1864 the Governors were assured that the district had at last been assigned (in 1863) and that the stipend of the perpetual curate was to be £100 a year, plus the £50 bequeathed by Lady Anne Holbourne. Mr. Short asked them to provide a house for a sexton and a curate but they considered both unnecessary. He thought there should be chapels of ease at Chadwick End and Bedlam's End and also at Balsall Street to cover the more outlying areas. The Governors postponed a decision on this.[7]

They then evidently had second thoughts, and at their usual August meeting in 1864 resolved that a cottage should be made for the sexton out of part of the Old Hall, where he was to live rent free, with a salary of £5 a year, which was to be £10 until the cottage was complete.[8]

Plans now followed with better than normal Governor-speed. Thomas Garner's architect's plan for a chapel at Balsall Street (St Peter's-to-be) was approved, and also a plan for making two bedrooms for the curate in the Old Hall. They were each to have an iron bedstead, washing stand, dressing-table and chest of drawers, and there was to be a sitting-room with table, chairs and writing table. The plan for the chapel proved too dear and modifications were suggested, but by 1869 the Old Hall was in three sections, the sexton's, curate's and the remainder as the court house as previously.[9] When St Mary's became a parish church thought was given to provision for the outlying areas, and eventually there were three daughter-churches, St Peter's (Balsall Street Chapel), St Chad's and St Richard's. St Peter's, situated near the growing population of Balsall Common, is the only one of the three to survive, and indeed thrive.

The Parish Breakfast

Just before the first World War, on 16 October 1913, a notable event took place in the Prayer Room at Temple Balsall—the first parish breakfast. Not only the first for Temple Balsall, but the first for any church in the whole of the country.

It was the brain-child of the vicar, the Rev. F.R. Fairbairn. Most of his congregation had walked or cycled some distance to come to early Communion, and Fairbairn thought it would welcome refreshment and an opportunity for the congregation to meet socially. It was a simple meal of bread, butter and marmalade, with cups of tea, and treacle on bread and margarine for the children. All the duties involved, preparing the meal, laying the tables and washing-up, were carried out by volunteers, and costs were met by a collection at the tables.

Some fifty or more attended, and it appears that eventually some of the residents in the Court were disturbed by the people passing to the Prayer Room, and the Governors said it could no longer be used for this purpose; they offered the use of the school instead, at a charge of half a guinea a time. This put it out of the reach of the congregation, and to highlight their grievance they held the next breakfast outside the gates opening on the vicarage drive. This ploy attracted the local press, who reported that the congregation of Temple Balsall was 'forced to have their breakfast on the roadside'.

The Old Hall was soon made available, and the breakfasts were held there for many years. Members of other churches sometimes came to see how it was organised, and the idea spread. The Silver Jubilee was marked by a service on 16 October 1938, and the 75th anniversary was celebrated by the Bishop of Birmingham, the Right Reverend Mark Santer, on 16 October 1988. The monthly gatherings are still held today, when coffee and biscuits are served. (From the Temple Balsall Archive, Book 7.)

Three Daughter Churches—St Richard's Church—Meer End

On 16 April 1928, the day of the Translation of St Richard, Bishop of Chichester, a service of thanksgiving for water was held at the well on the site chosen for the new church; prayers were said to ask that the well should be free from pollution, and the first sod for the church was ceremonially cut.[10] The building, designed by Father Downton, the priest in charge, was to be brick built, of two storeys, the upper room for parish use; it resembled a Tudor barn when complete.

It was dedicated a year later on 10 April, by J.H. Richards, Archdeacon of Aston, supported by the Rev. R.J.B. Colthurst, vicar of Hampton in Arden, described as 'the mother parish', though by this date Temple Balsall was the parish church of the district. St Richard's was intended primarily for the benefit of the Sunday School children ' from the remote rural areas of Meer End and Fen End'. It was built with money lent by the Birmingham Diocesan Sites and Building Fund on security given by a private benefactor (in fact by the Rev. F.M. Downton). The site was sold at a reduced rate by the Burton family of Chesterton Farm, Meer End. The architect was Mr. Frank Osborne of Messrs Osborne & Co., Birmingham, and the builders were George Deeley and Sons, a local firm.

Sixteen years later on St Richard's day (3 April 1946) a memorial crucifix in honour of Father Downton, 'the builder of the church', was dedicated, the funds being provided by his friends, largely organised by Mrs. Fairbairn, widow of the late vicar of Temple Balsall, the Rev. F.R. Fairbairn, who had donated the oak altar to the church.[11] It is clear that the church soon ran into financial difficulties,

100 St Richard's as it was when built in 1929. (Warwick CRO DR B/112/1; the poor quality of reproduction is due to the unavailability of the original photograph.)

101   St Richard's as it is today, a private residence called St Richard's House.

and fund-raising events were held, though to no avail. Father Downton impressed all the local people by his saintliness, and is said to have 'given his all for the church and died a pauper'.[12]

The church struggled on till the 1970s when the sad decision had to be taken to secularise the building and convert it into a dwelling house. The present owners are the third since the secularisation.[13]

St Chad's Church, Chadwick End

The fire insurance for the year 1921-2 for 'Chadwick End Chapel' (referring to the former school which was licensed for divine service and which also became known as St Chad's Church) gives an impression of a well-founded place of worship. Insured for £470 are 'seats, pulpit, font, reredos, screens, church plate, embroideries and textile fabrics, printed music, books, bells, a harmonium etc. Building of brick or stone and slated or tiled, and heated by a Tortoise stove'.[14]

But by 1949 repairs were urgently needed 'so that services can be resumed'. A long hiatus of almost six years now followed until 1955, when the restored church was opened 'as a venture of faith'. Optimism seems at first to have been justified, for services now became regular. By 1970, however, the state of the building was deteriorating and it was reported the next year that the numbers of worshippers were slowly dwindling.

102   St Chad's Church: interior. Christenings were held here. (Temple Balsall Archive.)

103   Chadwick End Church. St Chad's, said to seat about fifty people, but congregations dwindled until it was decided to dispose of the church. (The poor reproduction is due to the unavailability of the original photograph.)

Moves to sell off the church and adjoining Church House however seem to have galvanised local feeling as the sale became imminent. Members of the congregation offered to pay for repairs, and helped with the work; support between 1972 and 1976 was 'going from strength to strength' so that finally St Chad's was declared to be in good condition, with a new carpet and gate. Unfortunately the following year 'the congregation has dropped off', and in 1978 the new vicar was confronted with three abortive Sundays, and services were abandoned for a time. In 1980 a notice on the church door spelt the end. Services were suspended, and the sale of the church took place shortly afterwards, raising £20,000 for diocesan funds.[15] The church was demolished and a modern dwelling-house was built on the site.

St Peter's Church, Balsall Street East

In 1867 a Mr. Perkins offered a site for a chapel at Balsall Street, and a group of possible subscribers met and approved a plan produced by Mr. Garner the architect. This was found to be too expensive and modifications were suggested. Formal moves to convey the site to the Ecclesiastical Commission were followed by the building and the licence for the church in 1871.[16] The Governors of Temple Balsall contributed £200 towards the cost and, later, a further £25 to help liquidate the debt of about £60 still owing on the building.[17] It is an unpretentious structure of brick, a simple nave without aisles like the mother-church.

During the First World War, a group of local people had a thought to spare for their church, when 40 of them raised £34 towards a stained-glass window for the east end, with more funds promised, but it was not until 1955 that a legacy enabled the window to be installed and dedicated. Land for a parsonage was bought soon after the end of the war, and in 1923 the fire insurance was adjusted to include the installing of an Artesse stove in the church; the chapel was now dignified by its title of St Peter's Church, Balsall Street.[18]

St Peter's finally came of age in 1959 when, almost a hundred years after St Mary's, it became a parish church, and the following year the Rev. R.H. Barker was installed as vicar rather than 'priest-in-charge'.[19] The Rev. A.S. Montgomerie now ministers to a flourishing church; the parish magazine testifies to the liveliness of his parishioners.

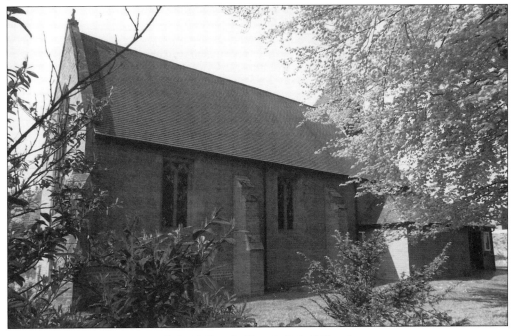

104   St Peter's Church, Balsall Street.

Chapter 23

Schooling for All Children
The 1870 and 1902 Acts

Increasing awareness of the importance of education led to two most important and far-reaching Acts of Parliament: both made universal education compulsory, the 1870 Act relating to the primary stage, and the 1902 Act to secondary education.

Existing voluntary schools, paid for by private subscription, were chiefly church schools, especially in the villages. They now (1870) had their earlier government grant doubled, and to fill the gaps not so provided, non-denominational schools, publicly controlled and funded, were planned. Two new local schools resulted in 1875 from this legislation: Chadwick End and Holly Lane (often called Balsall Street, rather confusingly) Schools. Both were primary schools, replacing the early Dame Schools (see Chapter 20). A third school was likewise built at Barston.

105   Holly Lane School in the snow, *c.*1875. (From C.A. Jones, *Balsall Street School: the first 75 years* (1988), by permission.)

106 Balsall Street School (now known as Balsall Common Primary School), 1913. (From C.A. Jones, *Balsall Street School: the first 75 years* (1988), by permission.)

The Governors made contributions to all these three schools from the funds of the Lady Katherine Leveson Charity, though they had originally opposed the building of Holly Lane, believing that there was already enough provision, and fearing that it might draw pupils away from Temple Balsall (the Lady Katherine Leveson School as it is now called).[1]

Difficulties arose before long. In 1884, only nine years after it was built, the Holly Lane (Balsall Street) School was in poor repair. Three deputies from the Governors visited it and decided that it was not worth adding to, but that a new school in two departments, one for mixed infants and one for older girls, for not less than 100 children should be built, together with a house for the schoolmistress.[2]

The Governors as a whole approved of these suggestions and applied to the Charity Commissioners for sanction to acquire a site and erect the proposed buildings. But in April 1886 a special meeting was called and a deputation of parishioners stated their views. They thought that as the schools at Balsall Street (*sic*) and Chadwick End had been built by subscription, they should be used as originally intended, that is, for infants up to eight years of age. Both schools were then being used as mixed and infants schools (three years before this, the Governors were concerned that the Girls' School at Balsall was not being so well-attended as before, since the girls preferred the mixed school at Balsall Street!). The parishioners thought the plans for new buildings were unnecessary. There was evidently a compromise, for by August that year the Master of the Hospital reported that Miss Jane Monteith had been engaged as mistress of the Infants' School at Balsall Street at a salary of £40 a year (and that Miss Wiseman, mistress at Chadwick End School, had asked for a rise).[3]

It is clear, however, that things went on much as before, for in 1887 a parish meeting was called, where the parishioners again asked the Governors to allow the

107   Balsall Common Primary School glimpsed through the railings.

school at Balsall Street to revert to its old status, and suggested that in special cases children over eight years old should be allowed to attend Chadwick End School.[4]

Yet another challenge awaited the Governors when their right to charge School Pence was questioned. The terms of Lady Katherine's will were invoked: she had only specified 20 poor boys. But then they had second thoughts and resolved that both schools should be carried on at their sole expense.[5]

After more hesitation, they decided that, pending re-organisation (meaning some extra building), both Chadwick End and Balsall Street Schools should be used as mixed and infants schools, and this appeared to have continued to the end of the century. By then the Local Education Authority (the County Council) was beginning to press for new central schools for the area, a theme which recurred from time to time long before it was carried into effect.

The great Act of 1902 must have brought considerable relief to the beleaguered Governors, for it meant that for Temple Balsall school, salaries, books, stationery and fuel were all to be paid by the Local Education Authority, to the tune of over £340 a year. But the coming of public provision and accountability could be a mixed blessing, for in 1904 the Director of Education, to much local indignation, proposed that Lady Katherine Leveson School should be re-organised, with mixed classes under a new head, a married man, dismissing the present head after his 24 years' service, and also the headmistress. The Civil Parish Council, formed 10 years earlier, raised strong objections to this on the grounds that the change would not be conducive to the morals of the children, many of them 14 years old and upwards. It was agreed in the end that the school should be split into two departments, keeping the same headmaster.[6]

In 1907 a public meeting was held at the *Saracen's Head* to discuss the Governors' offer to provide £1,500 and a site for a new church school to replace Holly Lane School which was grossly overcrowded. A deputation of the Parish Council had met the Warwickshire Education Committee concerning the project, and they reported back to the public meeting. The outcome, briefly, was this: the present Balsall Street (Holly Lane) School and site were not viewed favourably because there was not room for expansion. It seemed certain that the County Council (the L.E.A.), if compelled to provide more school accommodation, would choose a central site, and it would be at the expense of the ratepayers and therefore non-denominational. The Committee (of the Parish Council) urged that the Governors' offer be accepted, and at last a site was obtained in Balsall Street, and Balsall Street Council School, now called Balsall Street Primary School, was finally opened in 1913. The original school building in Holly Lane became a church room for St Peter's and was eventually demolished and replaced by the present Scouts/Guides Headquarters.[7]

The foundation of the Heart of England Comprehensive School in 1955, which is still expanding, completes the tally of educational provision in the area. The Heart of England School, for 11-18 year olds, celebrated its 40th year in 1998, the same year that the Sixth Form Centre opened in Leveson Block. From a small rural high school in the 1970s, with a student roll of less than 600, and a sixth form of 18, it has now grown to accommodate numbers exceeding 1,300, with a sixth form of 220. Courses cater for General National Vocational Qualifications (GNVQ) in Art and Design, Business Studies, Health and Social Care, Leisure and Tourism. Besides the usual A-Level courses, the subjects on offer include Computing, Music, Physical Education and Psychology. The prospectus reveals a most lively and progressive institution.

108 Heart of England School, Gypsy Lane, Balsall Common.

Chapter 24

The Water Supply at Temple Balsall

The supply of drinking-water at Temple Balsall must have been unsatisfactory for many years, but by the late 19th century the situation was clearly desperate. In 1887, one D. Willson, who had sunk the well at the Old Hall, informed the Bailiff that the substrata all inclined from the churchyard to the well, and if the water was contaminated it must be from the source, for the well was now puddled round with clay for its whole depth, and there was no chance of surface contamination.[1]

The Bailiff, for his part, reported that the drains from the women's wash-house had long been stopped up, and soap suds etc. had been running into the soft water cistern by the north door; also that the 'receptacle' (a soak-away?) into which all the slops were poured had also long been stopped up, and foul water was running back, partly into the well supplying drinking-water to the Hospital and schools, and partly into the soft water cistern under the north side of the Hospital. (Some forty years before, two great brick-built cisterns had been laid under the turf behind the two wings of the Hospital, to collect rainwater from the roofs; drains from the spouts were laid to convey the rainwater into the 'tanks' and pumps installed to draw the water off.)[2] An analyst declared the well-water unfit for drinking; the subsoil consisted entirely of loose gravel, and the contamination had been going on for a long time. In the meantime he advised them to empty and clean out the well, and then have a fresh analysis made.[3]

The well was cleaned and purified 'by a process used at Stoneleigh', but analysis showed that the water was still bad. The north side of the Hospital was re-drained, and in desperation, Mr. W. Gray, engineer to Birmingham Corporation Water Department was consulted. Presumably on his recommendation, a Mr. Blake of Accrington now visited the Hospital (in 1889) and proposed erecting a hydraulic ram. It is not clear where he thought of placing this, but in any case he was not able to find a suitable position; the next desperate resource was to employ a Mr. Mullins, water-diviner, who found a promising site which could supply the Hospital by gravitation; a well was sunk, but the quality of the water was poor.[4]

Two years later, the situation was, if anything, worse still. The Bailiff reported that there was illness at the Master's house, Temple House and the Old Hall. He was instructed to ask the Charity Commissioners if they would sanction the cost of providing a proper water supply for the Hospital out of capital. As if that were not enough, he had been instructed by the Solihull Sanitary Authority to disconnect the Hospital drains from the brook within seven days, for the brook was a tributary of the River Blythe from which the Corporation of Birmingham drew some of their water. He put out the suggestion that it might be possible to obtain a water supply from a deeper drain running through the gravel under the peat on Wroxall Abbey Estate and Priest Park Farm (Temple Balsall). It could be conveyed to the Hospital by gravity or a small ram on the line of the route, which would be much cheaper than pumping. The Governors decided to ask Mr. J.E. Willcox of Temple Row, Birmingham, to report on the best method of supplying water and give an estimate of the cost. That still left the problem of the sewage.[5]

By 1886 the water from the wells was still bad, and as late as 1904 they were still vainly sinking new wells, discussing the Wroxall Abbey plan, and possible difficulty with wayleaves. They had not been able to come to an agreement with Birmingham Corporation, but a gleam of hope appeared when the North Warwickshire Water Company began boring for water at Cuttle Pool Farm; the Governors applied to them for a possible supply to the Hospital but could get no definite

109 Unidentified, undated newspaper photograph of almswomen drawing their water from a well below the Old Hall, beyond the brook. Water from the wells near the Court was dangerous, unfit to drink in 1981 (CRO CR 1540/1, 474, 524). The well was dug in 1897 as a temporary relief, but it was not till 1914 that work started on provision of mains water (CR 1540/2, 163). (The poor quality reproduction is due to the unavailability of the original photograph.)

110 Pump for well at the rear of the old Hall. The churchyard is on rising ground above the well. (Watercolour from the Aylesford Collection, Birmingham Reference Library; Warwick CRO Pr Tem. chu., 1-6.)

answer out of them. The Rural District was asked to put pressure on the Company and this, combined with the appointment of a new Bailiff (Nigel L. Holbeche), prompted the Water Company to come up with an estimate of £600 for conveying the water main from Knowle to Temple Balsall. By 1912 the estimate had risen to £700 and the Charity Commissioners agreed that half the cost could come out of capital. The Education Foundation would be expected to pay the other half. Estimates for laying the water to the various buildings had to be considered, but at last, in 1914, an agreement with the Water Company was finalised, and work was to begin at once.[6]

The arrival of pure water must have made an enormous difference to the comfort and convenience of the people of the hamlet, to say nothing of their health. (For years, the schoolchildren had brought their own water in bottles.) The wonder is that so many had lived to such great ages on the well-water. It is likely, however, that nothing more than stand-pipes were installed at this date, for as late as 1919, perhaps in bad weather, from February to April, 'water was being carried to such Dames as needed it'.[7]

Chapter 25

The Court and the World Outside

In the 18th and 19th centuries, whilst life pursued its more or less even tenor within the shelter of the Court, the Industrial Revolution was gathering unstoppable momentum. Roads, canals, railways were all insistently developing. Temple Balsall, remote from manufacturing enterprises, came through virtually untouched. Sand-wiched between the turnpike road and canal from Birmingham to Warwick on the west, and the London-to-Birmingham railway and Warwick-to-Coleshill turnpike on the east, the integrity of the estate was stoutly maintained by the Governors, who yielded a mere 4½ acres to the London and North-Western Railway Company at Bradnocks Marsh in 1834 for the London to Birmingham line.[1] Shortly before this we find them registering their 'objections to the proposed canals', without giving any details.[2]

In general these great advances in communication seem to have had little impact on the Court, though Mary Powner's 'trifles of furniture' probably came from Trentham by linked canals to Birmingham and thence on the Birmingham-Warwick canal to Knowle, leaving about a mile and a half to cart by road to Temple Balsall. The Master might well have preferred to go to Birmingham by train rather than on horseback, and perhaps some of the Dames made the occasional trip.

The making of the Coleshill to Warwick turnpike, however, certainly entailed suffering to at least one cottager on Balsall Common some sixty years before; Samuel Swaine was ejected from his cottage by 'Messrs Payne and Chamber', and the case came up at Warwick Assizes in 1783.[3] Unhappily the Assize Rolls were destroyed, so the outcome of the case is now unknown.[4]

At no time is the contrast between Temple Balsall and the outside world greater than at the end of the 18th and the beginning of the 19th centuries. A series of bad harvests and a rising population led to a scarcity of food, record high prices and food riots in Birmingham which were only quelled by 80 special constables armed with staves, and the threat of military reinforcements.[5] The Dames of the Court were mercifully cushioned against undue hardship by substantial allowances 'owing to the scarcity', and in respect of the price of butchers' meat—over £34 in 1801, £28 in 1802

111 Miss Powell, former matron, forced to retire through failing eyesight, was taken in as an almswoman. Here she is standing before the Schoolhouse, *c*.1960. (Temple Balsall Archive.)

and £26 and £22 in the following two years were allowed by the Governors.[6]

(Another period of disturbances in Birmingham had its repercussion on Temple Balsall. In 1791 Dissenters [notably Joseph Priestley] were actively seeking parliamentary reform [and dangerously expressing sympathy with the French Revolution]. Violent opposers rioted, and burned and pulled down Dissenters' houses including Priestley's. To compensate victims of this riot a hundred rate was levied, and the Lady Katherine Leveson Charity, as representing the parish, was mulcted of 15 shillings in 1793 and £2 13s. 3d. in 1795.[7])

Besides special hardship allowances, the Dames had their regular bread and milk rations, to say nothing of the coal allowance (45 tons were ordered for the Court in 1806, for example, and similar amounts each year).[8] That the bread was no unmixed blessing is clear from entries in the Governors' Order Book for 1887: 'Bread for long had been inferior and many of the almswomen had been selling it at reduced rates and buying bread elsewhere. Also this made the women come to the road to collect it, and infirm ones had to pay others to fetch it.'[9] The Dames had a little money to buy better bread, and some unfortunates 'outside' (poor farm labourers from the overwhelmingly agricultural surroundings?) had been glad to put up with inferior bread if the price was right.

There can be no doubt that 'released from the exigencies of poverty and the necessity of carking and labouring for bodily sustenance' (as their prayer has it), the Dames' sojourn in the Court tended to prolong their lives beyond the normal average. The cases quoted in Chapter 14 must be viewed with some reserve, of course; Elizabeth Boston was said to be 108 years old at her death, and Elizabeth Page 94 the same year. In the next century Mary Green was credited with 97 years in 1810 and Mary Edwards 90, after 51 and 53 years each in the Hospital; as the latter figures are likely to be correct, it seems that they were admitted well before the age of sixty. It is clear that the 60-year rule was not inflexible, for out of 66 women admitted between 1841 and 1868, seven were under that age.

The compiler of the register of the candidates for the Hospital (1862 to 1909) was sufficiently struck by the Dames' longevity to enter the vacancies in the Court in 1886 thus:[10]

Elizabeth Arnold	died 16th October 1885	aged 89
Ann Allday	died 6th November 1885	aged 84
Ann Cranmer	died 10th December 1885	aged 80
Sarah Findon	died 15th December 1885	aged 95
Jane Weaver	died 31st December 1885	aged 87
Hannah Daffern	died 3rd January 1886	aged 80

515 years

Average 85.8333

Of these :

	Age at admission	Years in Court	At death
Elizabeth Arnold	75	15	89 (90)
Ann Allday	64	19	84 (83)
Ann Cranmer	-	-	80
Sarah Findon	58	36	95 (94)
Jane Weaver	82	6	87 (88)
Hannah Daffern	79	1	80

These women must have had a basic toughness to survive the hardships which qualified them for admission to the Court, but it is abundantly clear that, once admitted, their life expectation far exceeded the normal span. Elizabeth Arnold had almost reached the average life-span when admitted, but lived on in the Court for another 15 years. Ann Allday, admitted aged 64, would on average have lived another 12 years outside, but the Court gave her 19, and Sarah Findon's 36-year sojourn there certainly did her no harm! It was not until 1990, according to the official figures, that women of 65 could expect to live until they were 83.[11] Even Eliza Lewis, in spite of her ultimately fatal rheumatoid arthritis, lived to be 57 at a time when the average expectation of life for women was 55.[12] These are crude calculations, which could be multiplied many times over from the Temple Balsall registers, but they are compelling enough to demonstrate that life in the Court offered these women comparative ease at the end of their stressful lives, and many additional years in which to enjoy it.

The advent of Lloyd George in 1908 with his non-contributory Old Age Pensions Act for people over 70, probably caused a flutter in the Court, but when the provisions of the Act were spelt out, it was clear that the Dames did not qualify. Their yearly income was valued at £36 6s. 6d., whereas £31 10s. was the upper limit for qualification. The Dames' income was calculated thus:[13]

	£	s	d
Cash 6s. per week	15	12	0
Bread 6 lbs per week	6	17	0
Coal 2½ tons @ 36s.	4	10	0
Milk 23 gallons	4	3	0
Doctor	1	4	0
House 1s. per week	2	12	0
Clothes	1	0	0
	36	6	6

(properly 35 18 0)

(When a person's means were £21 a year, he was entitled to the full 5s. a week. For every 52s. 6d. a year the pension was diminished by one shilling a week until £31 10s. was reached, when no pension was payable.)

But not many qualifiers outside the Court could hope to reap the benefit for more than a very few years. In the census of 1901 for the Solihull Rural District, out of 7,917 females, only 152 had reached the ages of 70 to 75 (and that total would

112   In the back gardens. These plots were for the use of the almswomen or residents. Friends or relatives (with spades) help to till the ground under the eyes of the Dames. (Temple Balsall Archive.)

113 Mr. Frank Smith cuts the cake at his 90th birthday party in 1998. (Photo: Derek Robinson)

114 Resident of the Court, Mr. Frank Smith, aged 91, recently produced this rapid sketch to illustrate types of mushrooms (1998).

115 Nellie and May, residents of the Court, in 1987. May Williams (died 13 October 1990) and Nellie Jones (born 16 September 1909), still surviving, for many years inseparable companions, and universally known as 'Nellie and May'.

include the Dames of Temple Balsall), of whom less than half were likely to reach the 80s., and in fact those women reaching 65 in 1901 in England and Wales lived on average only to 77 years.

The Court Today

Of the 30 residents today (January 1999), 20 are over 80 years of age, and 10 of these are over 90 (two males and eight females); of the 30, six are males.

With the coming of the Welfare State, there is no longer the destitution of times past, but life can still bear harshly in other ways. The needs may be various: one resident no longer felt safe in her council flat as the area had changed; some have become frail and need care to continue their lives because of illness or the loss of a partner or carer; for some, the gradual loss of the ability to cope causes the move into care. Application may be made by the person in need, or their family or a friend, a social worker, the local doctor or nurse.

The Future

All in all, in can be seen that the Hospital, founded over 300 years ago, has carried out the intentions of the Founder, and, with fair weather, will continue to do so into the indefinite future, if not 'to the end of the World'.

Throughout the bustling pressures of the 19th century the Governors successfully warded off encroachments by road, rail and canal, and so, unscathed through the centuries, Temple Balsall sits amidst her green fields like some venerable oak, offering shelter and peace to the aged, and breathing a calm uplifting of the spirits to all who visit her.

LONG MAY SHE SO CONTINUE

Appendix I

The names in the Lay Subsidies of 1327 and 1332, Hemlingford Hundred, Balsall

LAY SUBSIDY: A tax levied on the value of movable goods of the laity on the authority of Parliament. Exempt were country dwellers whose movable goods were worth less than 10 shillings, and dwellers in cities, boroughs or ancient demesnes with goods worth less than six shillings. The tax varied from one grant to another, and between town and country. In 1327 country dwellers were taxed at 1/20th, town dwellers at 1/15th; in 1332 the ratio was 1/15th to 1/10th.

1327 (1/20th)	s	d	1332 (1/15th)	s	d
Richard Eberhale	5	9		8	7 ³/₄
Robert the clerk	4	1 ½		6	4 ¾
Adam de Farnhale		16 ½		2	2 ½
Geoffrey atte Berne	2	3 ½		2	9 ¼
Walter Hanekokes		22 ¾		1	8 ½
John Hagoneld	3		John Hauneld	2	10 ¾
Geoffrey de Farnehale		12	John the Smith	1	2 ¾
John Peche	2	9		2	7 ¾
Roger at the Cross		21		1	6 ¼
Adam Jaune	3	2			
Gilbert the Tailor	3	0	Ralph le Taillur	2	0 ½
Alice atte Fenne	2	6 ¾		3	0 ½
John Richardes	4	0 ½	John Richard	3	8
Alice de Bradenok	4	6 ½		3	0 ½
Ralph Segor	3	0	Ralph Rolves	4	3 ¼
Thomas Gamel	3	0		5	4 ½
John Gamel	3	0	John atte Grene	3	1 ½
John de Thotenhull		18		4	11 ¼
Adam Stevene		18		1	8
			Philip Foules	1	8
Total	53	3		62	9 ½

1327 Lay Subsidy: *Transactions Midland Record Society*, Supplement to vol.V (1901) (Indexes, vol.VI [1902]).

1332 Lay Subsidy: W.F. Carter, *The Lay Subsidy Roll for Warwickshire ... (1332)*, Dugdale Society Publications, vol.VI (1926), p.72.

Appendix II

View of Frankpledge
Some Possible Offences to be Inquired into

Breaches of the King's peace
Drawing of blood
Treasure found
Hue and cry raised and not followed up
Clipping of coins
Forcible oppression of women
Distraint of forbidden items, as, for example, beasts of husbandry
Diversion or obstruction of waters
Public roads or paths restricted or obstructed
Trespasses on the king's or lord's land
Harbouring of thieves
Strays not claimed after three days
Twelve-year olds who are not in a tithing
Withdrawing from a tithing without permission
Giving hospitality to a stranger without permission unless he come & go in one clear day
Christian usury
Bakers selling bread contrary to the assize
Brewers selling ale contrary to the assize
Possession of false gallons
Possession of false bushels, weights, toll dishes, false rods (measures)
Any matter touching the Crown or the liberty of the lord of the manor
Making a son into a clerk without permission
Cutting down trees without permission
Overburdening the common pasture of the village with the beasts of strangers without
    permission
Marrying one's daughter without permission
Allowing buildings to fall down on account of poverty

Appendix III

The Two Private Acts of Parliament Regulating the Lady Katherine Leveson Charity Warwick CRO DR B/23/77 Abridged Versions

1701-1702 (Queen Anne)

Trustees of the Charity to whom the manor of Balsall was devised:

Richard Newport, son of Lord Newport (later Earl of Bradford),
Charles Leigh, second son of Thomas Lord Leigh of Stoneleigh,
Sir William Bromley of Baginton, Knight of the Bath,
Sir Fulke Lucy of Henbury, co. Chester, knight,
Sir Bryan Broughton, William Sneyd, Robert Milward, John Offley,
Anthony Scattergood D.D., [all of Staffs], Randale Egerton Esq., of Bottley, Staffs,
Walter Heveringham of Aston near Stone, Staffs,
and Thomas Evetts of Balsall, gent. [bailiff of the manor]

From the profits of the manor:

they were to build a house of stone or brick as near to the church as convenient, as a hospital or almshouse for 20 poor women of good lives from the parish of Balsall; preference to be given to those in the greatest distress.

The almswomen were to receive yearly £8 and one grey cloth gown with the letters **KL** in blue cloth on the breast, to be worn continually; refusal to wear this meant ejection.

If there were not enough candidates from Balsall, suitable ones from Long Itchington, Trentham and Lilleshall might be selected.

A Minister to read twice daily from the Scriptures and to pray, either in the church or in the almshouse, with the almswomen, and to instruct them for the good of their souls. The Minister to have £20 yearly for this duty.

Thomas Evetts to oversee the almshouse, be the receiver of the rents and profits of the manor and defray the expenses. If there should be a surplus it was to be disposed among the almswomen. He was to be accountable to the trustees, who should nominate a successor on his decease.

> The trustees were to select the poor women, who were to receive the aforesaid benefits for life 'except for some notorious miscarriage' [misbehaviour], when the trustees might remove the offenders and replace them with other poor women.

> For the regulation of the Charity, the Bishop of Coventry and Lichfield should appoint 'Visitors and Governors' to assure that the intentions were observed by the trustees.

> The Minister appointed to read prayers should also teach 20 of the poorest boys of the parish of Balsall until they be fit to be apprentices, (he not taking anything from the boys' parents), for the said £20 a year.

In 1689 in order to increase the number of trustees, four of the original trustees granted by the process of lease and release:

> Thomas lord Bishop of Coventry and Lichfield, Sir Charles Holt, Sir Clement Fisher, Wm Bromley, Davenport Lucy, Thomas Fetherston and Wm Ebrall, their heirs and assigns, all the property which the original trustees had been enfeoffed with, to hold by them to the use of the thus increased number of trustees.
> [This was probably occasioned by the deaths of some of the original trustees.]

Forever hereafter there shall be eleven Governors, together with the Bishop of Coventry and Lichfield for the time being, in perpetual succession [they had power to co-opt on deaths or resignations, without the need for the legal process of 1689]; they were incorporated, with a common seal.

> The Governors might enlarge the number of almswomen but not lessen them below 20.
> They were to have £1000 out at interest as fire etc. insurance.
> Six Governors were to make a quorum.
> They were to have an anniversary meeting.

The Governors were to be immune to actions at law concerning the government of the Hospital.

1861 (Queen Victoria)

1   The number of almswomen to be 35.

2   The women to be appointed by the Governors, widows or spinsters, not less than 60 years of age, with a preference for those reduced from better circumstances, but providing that poor women disabled by illness or infirmity from maintaining themselves are eligible.

3   20 always to be from Balsall if qualified, the rest, if qualified, from Barston and Hampton in Arden and its hamlets.

4   Each almswoman to receive 6s per week, plus a reasonable quantity of bread, milk and coal, and a grey gown with **KL** on the breast, and a bonnet and a shawl.

5   The Governors to have power to expel or suspend for immorality, breach of rules, or if the woman becomes of unsound mind.

6   The Governors to employ a competent medical practitioner to attend on women and supply medicines or medical equipment, also one or more nurses when needed.

7   There were to be 4 pensioners each from Long Itchington, Trentham and Lilleshall.

8   Pensioners to have the same qualifications as the almswomen.

9   Each pensioner to have 8s a week paid half-yearly to the incumbent of their parish.

10 Pensioners to give up pension if they leave their parish. They may be deprived by the Governors for the same disqualifications as the almswomen.

11 The Governors may, with the approval of the Charity Commissioners, prescribe suitable regulations for the pensioners.

12 The boys' and girls' schools already established by the Governors to continue to be funded by the Charity. The Governors to make the rules.

13 Preference always to children resident in the hamlet of Balsall, but children from neighbouring parishes may be eligible for admission.

14 The church of St Mary to be maintained from Charity funds.

15 If St Mary's becomes a parish church, the minister is to be paid not over £100 out of Charity funds (in addition to the £50 payable under Lady Anne Holbourne's will), for performing services in the church, and visiting the inhabitants of Balsall providing he keeps a curate to assist him.

16 A clerk and sexton is to be paid £10 yearly.

17   The Master of the Hospital to be a clerk in Holy Orders of the Church of England, to be appointed by the Governors.

18   The Master to be paid £200 p.a., with rent-free house and garden and grounds.

19   The Master is to read prayers to the almswomen, visit them and give spiritual consolation, and exercise general superintendence over the Hospital and schools.

20   The Master may also hold the office of minister of the church at Balsall.

21   The Governors to have power to remove the Master for incapacity, immorality etc.

22   The Governors to appoint a competent Bailiff, with an annual salary of £100.

23   Surplus income, if any, to form a reserve fund for repairs or to increase the number of almswomen or pensioners or for the purposes of education.

24   Five Governors were to form a quorum.

25   The Governors may introduce regulations for the management of the Charity.

26   If there should be any doubt about any of these provisions, the Governors should apply to the Charity Commissioners for their advice, which if given shall be binding on all persons affected thereby.

Comment

The chief innovation of the 1861 Act was enlarging the number of almswomen from the 20 specified by Lady Katherine to thirty-five. They were to have 6 shillings a week, amounting to £15 12s. in place of the original £8. It is hard to say whether Clause 2, with its suggestions of preference for 'distressed gentlewomen', represents a new approach to the selection of candidates for the Hospital.

There was a proviso, in case St Mary's became a parish church, that the minister would be expected to visit the inhabitants of Balsall as part of his duties, and that he should keep a curate to assist him (? at his own expense).

The remaining provisions seem merely to affirm what had become traditional practice, as evidenced in the Governors' Order Books.

The Old Hall as Dwelling-House

Probate inventories survive of the goods of three householders who died in the Old Hall in the late 17th century. They were Christopher Evetts senior, who took the lease of the Temple Farm in 1660 and died in 1669, Francis, one of his sons, and Margaret Evetts, widow (? of Barlow Evetts). Christopher paid the Hearth Tax on three hearths in 1662/3 and 1664/5, then his son John (styled *Mr*, that is, of gentry status in the tax records) paid on five the next year. Perhaps John took over responsibility for the farm that year, letting his father retire from active life. There is a gap in the Tax records until 1669 when John again paid on five hearths

116   The Old Hall before the restoration of 1963. (Temple Balsall Archive.)

117 Piece of timber found during alterations in the Old Hall in the 1980s, carved with Lady Anne Holbourne's initials and the date of her death.

118   The Steward's Chair in the Old Hall. Manor courts were presided over by a steward (lawyer), acting for the lord of the manor. At Balsall his initials were carved on the splat of the chair at the beginning of his office. F.W.— Francis Wheeler 1775-1805; R.G.—Richard Gresley 1805-1838; J.W.W.—John Welchman Whateley 1838-1873; C.C.—C. Couchman 1873-1886; R.N.H.—Robert Neville Holbeche 1886-1911. In 1791 Robert Hester was paid 17s. for making an Elbow Chair for the Court Hall and repairing the old chairs in the same (Warwick CRO CR 112 Ba/181, Item 32).

for that year. Then Mrs. Evetts, widow (presumably of John, who died at Christmas 1669, and similarly accorded the title of *Mrs*) paid the tax on five until 1674 when the surviving records end.[1]

In January 1671 Thomas Evetts took on the lease of the Temple Farm with the manor house (the Old Hall), with the proviso that he must not sublet the house,[2] but it is clear that Lady Katherine soon waived this clause, for we find first Ann, John's widow, then by 1674, his brother Francis, paying tax on the hearths there. Thomas himself was paying hearth tax on a house in Oldich at that time.[3]

Francis, one of the brothers who had disputed the legality of his marriage, came to the Old Hall some time after 1674, and died there in 1681, followed by Margaret Evetts who died there in 1696.[4]

The following plan produced by the Royal Commission on Historic Monuments in England in 1993 is restricted to the medieval part of the building, the original hall (once open to the roof), omitting the later parlour (the west wing). The inventories cover the whole building, including the first floor. Whilst it is not possible to identify with certainty the ground floor rooms of the inventories with those shown on the plan, they nevertheless enrich our appreciation of the building and its uses.

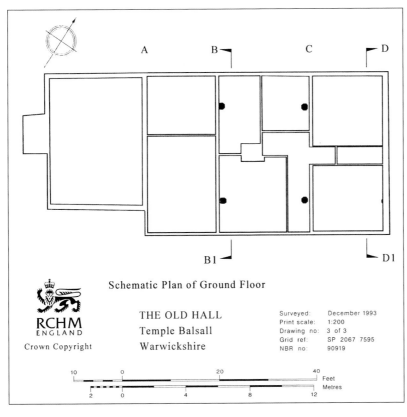

119 Schematic ground-floor plan of the Old Hall. (RCHME Crown Copyright © Reproduced under licence.)

Schematic Plan of Ground Floor

RCHM
ENGLAND
Crown Copyright

THE OLD HALL
Temple Balsall
Warwickshire

Surveyed: December 1993
Print scale: 1:200
Drawing no: 3 of 3
Grid ref: SP 2067 7595
NBR no: 90919

	Christopher (1)	Francis (2)	Margaret (3)
	GROUND FLOOR		
WEST WING	Parlour	Parlour	Parlour
HALL	Great chamber	hall	hall chamber
	kitchen	kitchen	kitchen
	cheese chamber	cheese chamber	cheese chamber
			the old kitchen
	cellar		the bacon cellar
	FIRST FLOOR		
WEST WING	chamber over parlour	chamber over parlour	parlour chamber
HALL	chamber over entry	chamber over hall	hall chamber
	next little chamber	the closet	
	men's servants chamber	chamber over the old house	chamber over kitchen
	little buttery	the other buttery	
		the cocklofts	cocklofts
	DETACHED BUTTERY		
		the best buttery	the buttery
	chamber over buttery		chamber over buttery

Not only was the upper space of the hall then utilised, but these first floor rooms were presumably ceiled over to make the 'cocklofts'. The buttery over the cellar (see Chapter 18) evidently had a chamber over it which was old Christopher's room, for it contained his clothes and his purse with money in it. (Numbers in brackets refer to the three separate inventories.)

Comment

The rise in the number of hearths from three to five may have been partly occasioned by Christopher's adoption of the chamber over the buttery—perhaps he had a hearth installed. The absence of hearths cannot be assumed from a lack of grates, andirons, etc. in the lists, for they are not consistent: Christopher's (1) and Margaret's (3) give no sign of a hearth in the parlour, but Francis' (2) notes a pair of andirons.

Contents of the House

Beds

(1) has five bedsteads, all equipped with feather beds (mattresses), pillows, curtains, valances, blankets, bolsters; one trundle (truckle) bed—with wheels so that it could be pushed under another bed in the daytime. In the ?servants' room there were one feather bed and one flock bed, presumably on the floor as there was no bedstead.

(2) has four bedsteads and one truckle bed much as in (1).

(3) has five bedsteads as above. In the ?servants chamber there were now two bedsteads, one feather bed, one flock bed and also one strike of malt and a mustard mill. There are no extraneous items in any other chambers.

Note: *All the beds are on the first floor.* The parlour, which in many houses contained a bed, here was kept as a 'reception room' in the modern manner, with a round table (1 and 2), 12 chairs (2), six forms and stools (3), a court cupboard (1 and 2), a carpet (2) and screen (1) and a pair of andirons (2).

Some Other Contents

In (1) 10 pairs of flaxen sheets (worth £4) and nine pairs of coarse sheets (that is harden or hempen [hessian] worth £1 10s.) hint at the rising fortunes of the family which yet has strong links with its yeomanry origins. Three spinning wheels in the cheese chamber (3) remind us that so much was home-made, though there is no loom listed anywhere. Perhaps Old Joan in her day (or other servants) wove for the family as well as weaving her own shifts (Chapter 14). Not only home-made, but home-grown, for the cocklofts held five and a half stone of flax, some 'hurds' (hemp) besides 20 pounds of wool and woollen yarn and nine pounds of linen yarn (3). Moreover, in the barn (1) is flax to the surprising value of £30 'watered and unwatered', indicating the early process of linen-yarn making.

Food

Cheese was a major part of their diet—half a hundredweight in (3), £2 10s. worth in (1), £2 5s. worth of cheese, peas and malt in (2), with beef and bacon featuring prominently as well.

Implements and Utensils
All the necessaries for making cheese, beer, bread and butter, and for salting down meat for the winter are present in all the lists. Out of doors, the barns contain wheat, barley, peas, oats and hay, and the livestock comprises cows, bull, sheep, pigs and horses. Implements of husbandry (ploughs etc.) are also listed, of course.

Special Items of Interest
Francis' inventory (2) notes two guns, pistols and holsters in the hall, with two swords and a belt. In the closet is a little table with books (a somewhat rare item), and London (delftware) and Ticknell ware 'with other necessaries', probably chamber pots (see Chapter 18 for the wares).

It is noticeable that items of luxury are few; Christopher has one silver bowl, one little silver jug and ten silver spoons, though there is a considerable amount of pewter—140 dishes and plates of this metal. Only Francis has glass bottles (? for wine) but there are no wine glasses. By the time the family left the Old Hall in 1740, their household goods had increased and gained in refinement considerably, though even then they did not reach the standard of the up-market family of Nottingham quoted in Chapter 18.

By the time the Rev. Thomas Ward visited Temple Balsall in 1830, all the partitioning and first floor had been removed from the hall, leaving only the parlour, which was used for the meeting of the courts, and the chamber over it. The hall proper, then in its early medieval form, open to the roof, was used as a lumber room.[5] Still later, in about 1850, a small smithy had been installed at the eastern end, and it was not until the late 19th century that the hall returned to use as a dwelling place, when the sexton's cottage and the curate's room were formed.[6]

Appendix V

Memorial Inscriptions in the Church

(Stones in floor unless otherwise stated. Each begins with 'In memory of' or 'To the memory of'; names only given here.)

1 Plaque on wall: Brigade colours of St John's Ambulance Brigade deposited 1940.

2 Plaque on wall: In memory of Insull John Burman, Temple House; fell at El Alamein 2nd November 1942, aged 24 years.

3 Elizabeth, wife of Joseph Boultbee Esq., of Springfield House, Co. Warwick, d 5 May 1822.

4 Jane, relict of Wm Evetts, gent, daughter of Ralph Edge, Esq., of Strelley, co. Notts. Born 31 Jan. 1731, d 27 Dec. 1789, aged 58 years. Nephew Thos Edge, Esq., caused this stone to be inscribed.

5 Wm Evetts, gent, d 18 July 1773 aged 32.

6 Mary Harrold, d 13 Sept., 1819, aged 88, Matron of this hospital 17 years.
Sarah Harrold, sister, d 1st November 1832. Matron 15 years.

7 Susannah Harrold, died 20 July 1800, aged 74. Matron 26 years. [figure 6 indistinct]

8 William (?Bacus) ... 13, d Sept. 8, 1750, aged 38.

9 Thomas Evetts, 2nd son of Barlow and Sarah Evetts, born 25 Mar. 1744, d 17 Aug. 1781, aged 37.

10 Aliss Elizabeth Bott, d 1 Nov. 1773, aged 48.

11 Wall Marble: Elizabeth Boultbee, uxor Joseph Boultbee, d 5 May 1822.

12,13,14 are beneath cupboards and not available for recording.

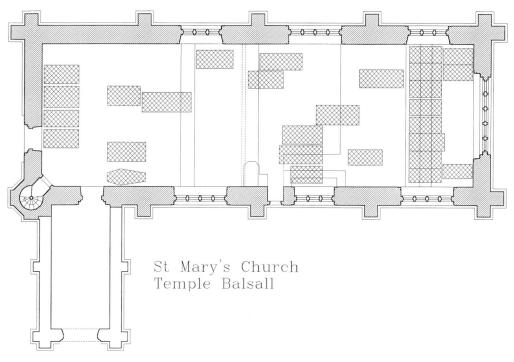

120 Tombstones: approximate positions as plotted in 1849. In the nave, from the 18th, 19th, 20th centuries, but the anonymous ones in the sanctuary could be much older. (Warwick CRO CR 1540/ 3/13: '1949 Blank Plan of Floor'; drawing, David Warren.)

15 [Translated from the Latin] Margaret Saunders, daughter of John Huntbach of Shoc(?) co. Staffs gent, m. Wm Saunders of Shareshill co. Staffs, 2 dau. Maria and Jana, (? . .) m. Thos Evetts of Warwick, gent. ? second m. Ralph Edge of Nottingham, Esq., D 27 Nov. 1725 aged 66. Wm Saunders d 30 May 1727, aged 72

16 Henry Couchman, architect, b. 19 Jan 1738 NS, in par. of Ightam, Kent, d. in Temple House 20 Jan. 1803 [more under furniture].

17 Susanna Barnes, relict of Thomas Barnes of Swanscombe, Kent, b. 28 Aug.1696 NS d. at Temple House 2 Jan 1781 age 85. She left issue [stone missing]

18 Wall marble to Mrs Susannah Harrold (see No. 7).

19 Wall plaque: Henry Couchman, d. at Temple House 29 Dec. 1838

20 Wall plaque: Susannah Barnes, relict of Henry Couchman, born 9 Nov 1737, d at Temple House 24 Mar 1804, aged 64.

21 Barlow Evetts, gent, son of Thomas and Mary Evetts, d. 5 June 1767, aged 46.

22 Mary late wife of Thos Evetts, gent, d. 9 June 1736, age 49.

23 Thos Evetts, d 19 . . and Charles ?Lo . . . . . . Ann his wife 2nd Aug ...

24 Thomas and Mary Cattell of Balsall Lodge ... by Ann their only child ... Her father d
    Aug 16 1846 aged 83. He was the youngest child of Richard Cattell of Balsall Lodge,
    born 1701, d 1761, eldest son of William Cattell of Balsall Lodge, eldest son of Wm
    Cattell of Balsall Lodge born 1663, d 1725. Both of whom left a widow and 7 children.
    Her mother d 2 May 1842, aged 78, 2nd daughter of Thos and Dorothy Bellamy of
    Haseley House, co. Warwick.

25 Mrs Ann Evetts, wife of Thos Evetts, gent, d. 7 Jan. 1776 aged 84.

26 Sarah wife of Barlow Evetts, d. of Thomas Webb, d. 27 Feb. 1757, aged 4?.

27 Inscription in window over west door to Joseph Boultbee and Elizabeth, ux.

Appendix VI

Masters of the Hospital

The appointment, length of service and deaths of the Masters of the Hospital are recorded.[1]
They are written in Latin as seemed fitting to their status of clerks in Holy Orders.

ROBERT CHAMBERLAIN
died 21st March 1696/7, the 19th year of his office.

PAUL LOWE
elected and admitted 27th May 1697; died 21st April 1722, after 25 years in office.

WILLIAM PHELPS
elected in his place 3rd August 1722; died April 1749 after 27 years in office.

THOMAS DADLEY
succeeded 20th May 1749; resigned after 50 years in office.

JOHN SHORT
elected in his place 13th October 1798; died 12th March 1855,
after 57 years in office and 87 years of age.

JOHN HOLBECHE SHORT
(John's only surviving son) admitted 4th April 1855; died in office.

F. R. FAIRBAIRN
elected 4th August 1902; resigned.

ROBERT W. BALLEINE
admitted 17th September 1931; resigned.

HENRY MILTON CRABB
admitted 8th June 1936; died.

The Reverend Canon ERNEST DUGMOR
admitted 17th March 1942; resigned 11th February 1948.

ALFRED ERNEST PALMER
admitted 1948; resigned 31st December 1959.

FRANCIS PALGRAVE BROWN
admitted June 1960; resigned 1966.

MICHAEL WALLS
admitted 1966; resigned 1974.

ROY VERNON ALLEN
admitted 1974; resigned 1978.

KEITH CHARLES JARRATT
admitted 1978; resigned 1982.

RICHARD WATSON WILLIAMS
admitted 1982.

It is a remarkable fact that the two John Shorts, father and son, covered over one hundred years at the Court, and with Thomas Dadley, over one hundred and fifty years between them.

[1] CRO DR (B) 36/5; Mr Geoffrey Burman, a Governor of the Charity, has kindly brought the list up to date.

Bailiffs of the Lady Katherine Leveson Charity

The Evetts Dynasty
(six generations from father to son)

THOMAS	From 1674. Made a Governor. Died 1696.
BARLOW	From 1696. Died 1711.
BARLOW	From 1711. Died in 1717 of tuberculosis.
THOMAS	From 1718. Elected Governor in 1738 and retired.
BARLOW	From 1738. Died 1757.
THOMAS	From 1757. Died 1765.
MRS ANNE EVETTS	Widow of Thomas. (Their son Thomas was then only four years old). From 1765. Died 1776.

Later Bailiffs

HENRY COUCHMAN	appointed in 1776 in place of Mrs. Evetts, but 'if her son be appointed at the proper age, Couchman is to resign'.[1]
HENRY COUCHMAN (junior).	From 1802.
CHARLES COUCHMAN	From 1838.
ROBERT NEVILLE HOLBECHE	From 1886.
NIGEL LAURENCE HOLBECHE	From 1911.

[1] Warwick CRO CR 1342/1, p.246. But Thomas did not take up the post and the Evetts succession came to an end.

Appendix VIII

Rules for the School at Temple Balsall

Warwick CRO CR 1540/1, pp. 268-70.

Prompted by the 1861 Act of Parliament which asserted the right of the Governors 'to pre-scribe suitable rules for the management of the Charity'; they laid down afresh the rules for the School and Hospital in 1862.

1 It was to be open to all the inhabitants of Balsall between the ages of 5 and 15 subject to the approval of the Master and at least one Governor.

2 Children to come clean in person and dress on pain of forfeiting three tickets[1] or some other punishment.

3 The school to be open from Lady Day [25 March] to Michaelmas [29 September] from 9 a.m. to 12.30 and 2 p.m. to 4.30 p.m. and from Michaelmas to Lady day from 9.30 a.m. to 12.30 and 2 p.m. to 4 p.m.

4 It was to open every morning with Prayers and everyone who is late is to forfeit a ticket and be placed at the bottom of the class. Prayers to be said at end of School.

5 A Register is to be kept by the Master or Mistress of the daily attendance of scholars, noting progress and behaviour of each.

6 A register of weekly attendance is to be given to the Master of the Hospital once a week.

7 Children must attend regularly. If absent without leave, except in cases of sickness, they will be liable to be dismissed and will not be admitted without a fresh order of admission.

8 There will be a holiday every Saturday, a week's holiday at Whitsuntide, a fortnight at Christmas and a month at Harvest (the time to be fixed by the Master of the Hospital). In fact the Governors ordered that the holidays for 1881 should be during haymaking rather than corn harvest time. (*Ibid.*, p.369.)

9 Books and writing materials must be provided by the Parents. They may be purchased from the Schoolmaster or Schoolmistress at reduced prices.

10 Every child admitted to the Day Schools may also attend the Sunday Schools.

11 Children of Farmers, Shopkeepers and others above the class of Labourers to pay two-pence a week in advance.

[1] It has not been possible to elucidate the system of tickets.

Appendix IX

Some Customs
Affecting Temple Balsall Villein Tenants
Under the Hospitallers and Later

* The youngest son inherited the land, or failing sons, the youngest daughter (as late as 1657—Warwick CRO CR 112/Ba 413).

* When a tenant died, after his debts and funeral expenses were paid, his movable goods and chattels were divided into three, one part going to the lords of the manor as a death duty (called an 'obit'), another part to the wife, and the third part to children if any. If there was a wife but no child, they were divided into two, one half for the wife, one half to the lords. If there was neither wife nor child, all went to the lords (*Calendar of Patent Rolls*, 20 Richard II, Pt III, pp.112-3).

* Women holding land could not marry without licence of the lords of the manor. Elizabeth Bradnock paid 5 shillings for a licence to marry Thomas Fox on 8th October 1657 (Reference as above).

* Any woman fornicating in her widowhood forfeited the lands she held in right of her late husband to the lords of the manor. From a court roll of Thomas Docwra, Prior of the Hospital of St John ... Temple Balsall (1514), translated from the Latin: 'Elena Rowlls, late the wife of William Roulls [sic] forfeited a messuage called Plowplace *because she had sexual congress with William Towers in her widowhood contrary to the custom of the manor there ...*' (Photo: Temple Balsall Archive, otherwise unprovenanced.) By the time of the Survey of the Manor of 1657, the forfeiture was to last only until she paid a fine (unspecified) to the lord of the manor. (Dugdale's *Antiquities*, vol.II, p.967)

* If any young woman tenant conceives a child out of wedlock she must come before the manor court and bring a 5 shilling fine and a purse worth one penny and a half and be formally re-admitted to her land.

* Disputes between tenants or between tenants and the lords involving less than 40 shillings must be settled in the manor court held every three weeks in the Old Hall.

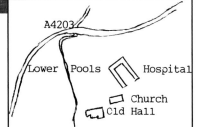

121 Remains of old fishponds. The unnamed brook below the Old Hall flows north under the A4203 road bridge to the River Blythe. Shortly before reaching the bridge, the brook takes a pronounced right-angled bend, the result of the original damming up to form the fishponds. The remains of these can be seen at either side of the brook when it floods and the waters begin to subside, as rectangular outlines. They were called 'Lower Pools' in 1759 (as marked on the map, based on Tomlinson's map of that year, Warwick CRO CR 621/6).

* Once a year the tenants must pay a duty called 'Take Silver', that is, one penny for every year-old pig, a halfpenny for every six-month pig, one pig being allowed free.

* If a tenant have a good mare it must be mated with the lords' stallion, and if a colt were born the lords were to have the option of buying it fourpence cheaper than anyone else. The lords provided a bull and a boar to service the tenants' cows and sows.

* If a tenant's lands had ponds or pools he was free to fish therein but where a river ran through his grounds he could fish in it, provided he had only scoop to ladle and a small spade to make a dam and also provided he did no great damage. He could take small fish such as perch and loach, but must leave the lords' fish (probably trout).

* Making the lords' hay: 33 tenants had to make hay on Balsall Meadow, and were given 7½ pence, 9 bakings of bread, 2½ stone of cheese and a wheaten loaf; 32 other tenants were to make hay on Temple Meadow, with the same reward, and the same for Chadwick and Hospital Meadows. At Christmas, Easter and Whitsuntide they were entitled to bread and cheese and ale at the Old Hall, *'sufficient for honest persons'*.

(Source except where stated: Warwick CRO Z146/2, William Dugdale's Ms copy of Balsall Custumal of 1548).

Appendix X

The Modernising of the Court

In 1963 Nicholas Brown was installed as Vicar and Master of Temple Balsall, and there began the great modernisation of the Court. Central heating was installed in all the flats, and each was provided with its own toilet and bath; brick firebreaks were built in the roof space, which until then had been a draught-channel through which fire might have burned unimpeded. These works cost over £50,000. Major alterations to the Master's House were also carried through at a cost of another £10,000; help towards these costs came from Meriden Rural District Council. (Source: Temple Balsall Parochial Church Council Minutes, 1948-1983.)

The Court and School Today

Now, both men and women, married or single, may apply for accommodation at the Court. The criteria have been relaxed: not all the present residents are Christian or poor, and a wider range of parishes is now included in the 'Area of Benefit':

Parishes in the County of Warwick

Ashow	Haseley	Rowington
Baddesley Clinton	Hatton	Shrewley
Beaudesert	Honiley	Stoneleigh
Beausale	Kenilworth	Tanworth-in-Arden
Bushwood	Lapworth	Wroxall
Claverdon	Preston Bagot	

Parishes in the County of West Midlands

Balsall	Castle Bromwich	Kingshurst
Barston	Chelmsley Wood	Meriden
Berkswell	Fordbridge	
Bickenhill	Hampton in Arden	

and Ward No.2 (formerly Knowle) in the Metropolitan Borough of Solihull

Residents are registered with their General Practitioners and are entitled to medical and nursing care under the National Health Service. Doctors and District Nurses visit the Court.

*

It is hoped that residents should have a home in the Court for as long as they need it.

*

There are 30 completely self-contained flats, to which residents are encouraged to bring their own furniture; five are suitable for couples. Common rooms are there for community activities. A guest room is there for relatives and friends of the residents to stay for a short visit.

*

There is a modern fire detection system and residents can call on a member of staff in an emergency.

*

The Parish Church of St Mary is within the grounds of the Court and is closely associated with the life of the Court.

*

'Sheltered Housing' is provided in the first-floor flats. Those who choose this pay a weekly 'maintenance charge' which covers the cost of the flat, central heating and the help of Matron or her staff. They may pay for and take their meals in the dining room if they wish. Twenty people are now in 'sheltered housing'.

*

Residents in the first-floor flats may be able to move to the ground floor if they need to, as vacancies occur. There they will have full Residential Care. Eleven people at present occupy these flats.

*

Some may choose Residential Care in the first place, and are given ground-floor flats. For them, meals are provided and there is assistance for heavy laundry and cleaning. An overall charge covers the cost of meals, electricity and extra staff assistance.

*

In either case, residents are free to come and go as they wish; the Governors and staff hope to relieve them of worry so that they can continue to live as active and varied lives as possible.

*

122 Fireplace with oven in each almshouse, before the modernisation (Temple Balsall Archive).

123 Bath used by all the residents before the modernisation (Temple Balsall Archive).

Charges

These are assessed each year by the Governors of the Court. In some cases part or all of the charges may be paid by the Solihull Metropolitan Borough Housing Department or the Department of Health and Social Security.

No applicant is refused because he or she cannot afford the charges.

*

Notice of Leaving

If a resident decides to leave the Court, one month's notice is required. On the rare occasions when the Governors have to ask a resident to leave, a month's notice is also given.

*

Applications

These are considered by a Committee of the Governors, who decide priority on the basis

124 Mr. Charles Seymour Watts and his wife Frances Eleanor in their flat, about 1978. Charles died in 1985, Frances in 1990.

of the greater need. A successful applicant will be invited to stay for a few days before deciding to come and live at the Court.

The School Today
(The Lady Katherine Leveson Primary School)

The modern school is a Church of England Aided School for up to 100 boys and girls, and children are accepted from all areas.

*

The teaching is aligned to the National Curriculum. Two classes are for the Infants, who spend three years getting a good grounding in the three Rs. They move up at the age of 7+ to the two Junior classes where they spend the next four years preparing for Secondary School Education.

*

Each child is taught individually, discipline is good, and there is a happy relationship between teachers and children.

*

There is a wide range of creative activities, a full P.E. programme and an active Parent—Teacher Association. Every classroom has a computer, and an extensive Science and Technology programme operates throughout the school. There are dining facilities and meals are cooked on the premises.

The School Offers

Small classes, experienced staff, up-to-date technology
Athletics, football, rugby, netball, cricket, rounders
Weekly swimming at Tudor Grange Pool, regular educational visits
Development of intellectual and creative abilities.

Notes

Prologue

1. E.g., Helen Nicholson, *Templars, Hospitallers and Teutonic Knights …* (Leicester University Press, 1995); (hereafter, 'Nicholson').
2. In Jonathan Riley-Smith, *The Knights of St John in Jerusalem and Cyprus, 1050-1310* (1967), pp.33-45; (hereafter, 'Riley-Smith').
3. L.B. Larking and J.M. Kemble, *The Knights Hospitallers in England* (Camden Society, LXV, 1857), p.lxiv; (hereafter 'Larking').
4. Seven canonical hours.
5. Larking *passim*.
6. It was laid down in 1206 that food and drink should be good enough to be tolerated by the brethren of the house. Riley-Smith, p.212.
7. Riley-Smith, p.214.
8. *Ibid.*, p.253.
9. *Ibid.*, pp.255, 257.
10. Larking, pp.lxix-lxxi.
11. Riley-Smith, pp.267-71.
12. Riley-Smith, p.235. In 1179, the Master of the Hospital, appealing for alms, promised 1, 000 masses throughout the world.
13. *Ibid.*, pp.242-6, 384, 440.
14. Larking, pp.4, 52
15. *Ibid.*, pp.64, 28, 35, 99, 197.
16. *Ibid., passim*
17. *Ibid.*, pp.40, 58, 62.
18. Nicholson, p.74, and see Eileen Gooder, *Temple Balsall—The Warwickshire Preceptory of the Templars and their Fate* (Phillimore, 1995), p.110; (hereafter 'Gooder'). At their trial the Templars declared that they were unlettered men, ignorant of the law and did not know how to defend themselves.
19. See below, Chapter 4.

Chapter 1

1. Gooder, pp.58-61.
2. *Calendar of Close Rolls 1327-1330*, p.234.
3. Larking, pp.215-20.
4. Larking, pp.lxxi-lxxii.
5. *Ibid.*, pp.212-13.
6. *Ibid.*, p.133.
7. *Ibid.*, p.22.

8. *Ibid.*, p.129.
9. Gooder, pp.50-63; Larking, pp.134-6, 140, 147, 160, 167, 172, 183, 186.
10. Larking, p.5.
11. Prologue pp.1-4.
12. Larking, pp.112, 125-6.

Chapter 2

1. Larking, p.3.
2. PRO E358/19 and *Calendar of Patent Rolls, 1307-13*, p.132. 23 June 1309, Edward II issued a writ from Chelvrescote (Chilverscoton).
3. Larking, pp.179-81.

Chapter 3

1. *Victoria County History, Warwick*, IV (1947), pp.88-90; (hereafter 'VCH').
2. PRO E 358/19, Rot 43 dorse.
3. Gooder, pp.65, 71 for early chapel, and early form of the Old Hall.
4. PRO E 358/18, 19, 20.
5. Gooder, pp.56-7, 82-6.
6. See above, Prologue p.2.
7. N. Pevsner, *The Buildings of England, Warwickshire*, with Alexandra Wedgwood (1966), pp.431-2.
8. William Dugdale, *History of the Antiquities of Warwickshire* (1730), (2 vols), vol.II, p.968; (hereafter 'Dugdale'). He was writing in 1656, before the 1663 restoration.
9. See below, Chapters 8 and 12.
10. Rev. H.T. Tilley and H.B. Walters, *The Church Bells of Warwickshire …* (1910).

Chapter 4

1. PRO, *Calendar of Patent Rolls, 1391-96*, p.525; *1396-99*, pp.112-13.
2. M. McKisack, *The Fourteenth Century* (Oxford, 1959), pp.407-22.
3. J. Stow., *The Survey of London* (1598), Everyman's Library (1912), p.387.
4. The Statutes of 25 Edward III (1351) and 1 Richard II (1371) concerning rebel villeins disobeying their lord.
5. Sir Edwin King, *The Knights of St John …* (1934), p.xvii, gives Brother Walter Grendon as head of the

Order 1400-1416, but the Patent Rolls for 1396 describe him as 'now Prior'.

6   *Cal. Pat. Rolls 1396-99*, pp.112-13.

Chapter 5

1   Warwick CRO CR112 Ba 363, 518, 519, the earliest rolls. Later rolls CR112 Ba 364-382 (1413-1624) would repay study by later historians.

2   John Gerveys, the lord's bailiff, conversant with the law as would be expected.

3   Strictly, the punishment in the view of frankpledge was a fine, not open to alteration. In the manor court it was called a *misericordia* translated as an 'amercement', because it was possible for the jury to be merciful and reduce the amount.

4   PRO JUST3/140, m.1, dorse, Gaol delivery roll.

Chapter 6

1   *VCH*, II, p.101; Sir George Clark, ed., *The Oxford History of England, the Fifteenth Century, 1399-1485* (E.F. Jacob, 1961), pp.556, 561, 569.

2   *VCH*, II, p.101.

3   Dugdale, II, p.965.

4   PRO STAC 2/33/40.

5   *VCH*, II, p.101; PRO STAC/Henry VII/File 59/1.

6   Protracted Star Chamber Proceedings, e.g. PRO STAC 1/50, 1/59; STAC 2/12, 2/17/401/8, 2/26/175.

7   PRO STAC 2/12.

8   Right of sanctuary: most churches had a limited right (40 days) but some had a special charter or licence to offer a more extended refuge. Knowle church was one such. Evidence of the use of the Sanctuary, including by alleged murderers, and a reference to the 'warden of the Sanctuary in Knole' is in *Letters and Papers of Henry VIII*, IX, p.190; XII, Pt I, p.228. Knowle must have been fairly widely known for two murderers from Inkberrow (Worcs.) sought refuge there, as well as a thief who had robbed an innkeeper in the Strand, London. *Ducatus Lancastrie Calendar of I.P.M.*, vol.I, p.113.

9   Sir George's supporters included: Henry Porter of London, gent., Thomas Benford of Claverdon, gent., John Clarke of Balsall, the younger, husbandman, Philip Ebrall, husbandman, Thomas Marche, husbandman, Fouke Lyngham of Coughton, husbandman, Thomas Fyssher of the same, yeoman, Thomas Ferrar, John Goodnall and Wm Pen of Barston, weaver, and Thomas Bryan of Balsall, collier.

10   PRO STAC 2/26/175.

Chapter 7

1   *VCH*, IV, p.88.

2   Second Governors' Order Book, Warwick CRO CR 1540/1, p.194. I am indebted to Mr. C.R. Humphery-Smith for the information about Revel land.

3   Dugdale, II (1730), p.969. Identifications have been made with the aid of J. Fairbairn's, *Crests of Great*

Britain and Ireland, vols.I and II (1860).

4   *Letters and Papers of Henry VIII*, vol.VIII, p.936.

5   *Ibid.*, vol.III, pt. 2 (1867), p.1192; Sir Edwin King, *The Knights of St John in the British Empire* (1934), pp.90, 100-3, 105, 113.

6   *Letters and Papers of Henry VIII, Addenda*, vol.I, pt.1, II, no.1693 (1545).

Chapter 8

1   PRO E315/361, ff.15-20. A photocopy of this is at Warwick CRO—Z146/3.

2   Gooder, pp.67-71.

3   Warwick CRO CR 621/6, Tomlinson, 'Plan of the Temple Balsall Charity estates in the manor of Balsall, 1759'.

4   G.M. Trevelyan, *English Social History*, 3rd impresssion (1945), p.157.

5   PRO E315/361, ff.19, 19v, 20.

Chapter 9

1   PRO E315/361, ff.15v, 18, and Warwick CRO Z146/3.

2   T. Tomlinson, 'Plan of the Temple Balsall Charity Estates in the manor of Balsall, 1759', gives Little, Far and Lower Park, Boggy, Middle and Great Park, Lime Tree Park, Gravely Park, Park Lays and Park Corner, Warwick CRO CR621/6.

3   Gooder, pp.12, 13, 53.

4   See Note 3.

Chapter 10

1   Stowe's *Survey of London* (Everyman edn, 1929), p.387.

2   This did not, of course, disturb Lord Dudley's title.

3   *Calendar of Patent Rolls*, 2-3, Philip and Mary, pt.II, pp.34-35. For a discussion of the mill site see Gooder, pp.78-80.

4   *VCH*, IV, p.88; Dugdale, II, p.968.

5   Alan Kendall, *Robert Dudley, Earl of Leicester* (1980), pp.145-9.

6   Arthur Collins, ed., *Letters and Memorials of State* (London, 1746), vol.I, pp.70-5.

7   Anon., *The Italian Biography of Sir Robert Dudley, knight* (London, published by Chapman and Hall, 1849), Warwick CRO C920 DUD, pp.1-3; (hereafter *Italian Biography*). This volume also contains the portraits: Douglas, Lady Sheffield, Sir Robert Dudley, Duchess Dudley, and Lady Katherine Leveson, with their captions as given here, facing p.51, opposite title page, facing p.85, and facing p.105.

8   *Ibid.*, p.4.

9   *Dictionary of National Biography*.

10   *Italian Biography*, p.2.

Chapter 11

1   *Italian Biography*, p.87; Burke's *Peerage and Baronage* (hereafter *Peerage*), p.1,470.

2. *Peerage*, p.1,470; *Italian Biography*, p.89.
3. *Italian Biography*, p.99.
4. *Ibid.*, pp 87-9.
5. Dugdale, II, p.968; *VCH*, VI, p.126. Vouchee—a person summoned to court; recovery—the recovery of the right to a property by decree, verdict, or judgement of a court.
6. Warwick CRO CR Ba112/177/1 and 2, miscellaneous bundle. Lady Katherine's seal to her licence to Thomas Evetts to sublet half his farm (Temple Manor Farm), 1671. She uses the Earl of Warwick's crest, the Bear and Ragged Staff.

Chapter 12

1. Dugdale, II, p.968 'in her lifetime'; writing in 1656, he described the church as 'very ruinous'; *VCH*, IV, p.88, 'in 1662 it was reroofed and restored by Lady Katherine Leveson and Lady Anne Holbourne', but no source for this is given.
2. Warwick CRO CR112 Ba 538
3. Watercolour (1), Warwick CRO DR(B) 23/76/1; (2) CRO PV TEM Chu 3.
4. Lady Katherine's will: Warwick CRO CR 1540/6.
5. Church plate donated to Temple Balsall, from: S.A. Jeavons, 'Church plate of the diocese of Birmingham', in *Transactions and Proceedings of the Birmingham Archaeological Society*, vol.81, Plates 8a and 8b.
6. Warwick CRO CR 112 Ba 413.
7. For a list of the Bailiffs, see Appendix VII.
8. A loose paper in the front of 'The Hospital Order Book No. 3' [begins 1893, ends 15 July 1957] Warwick CRO CR 1540/2.
9. [Endorsed 'Prayer K. L.'] Hospital Order Book No.3, f.2, Warwick CRO CR 1540/2; another copy in DR (B) 36/5, f.2.

Chapter 13

1. In Warwick CRO CR 112/177/1, misc. bundle; post-1674 as Lady Katherine is described as deceased.
2. *VCH*, VIII, pp.431, 460-1.
3. In Warwick CRO CR 112/177/1, misc. bundle.

Chapter 14

1. PRO Augmentation Office Misc. Book, cliv, p.135.
2. See above, p.**xxx**.
3. Warwick CRO DR (B) 36/5 Register of the almswomen (not paginated).
4. I am indebted to Mr. Geoffrey Burman for the loan of this letter.
5. First Order Book, p.39, 29 June 1704; p.51.
6. *Ibid.*, pp.67, 89, 91, 97; expulsions in fact seem to be rare events—Mary Woodward (above) being the single instance recorded in over a hundred years.
7. *Ibid.*, p.240, 17 September 1774; 14 August 1800.
8. *Ibid.*, p.118.

9. *Ibid.*, 25 October 1776.
10. *Ibid.*, October 1783.
11. *Ibid.*, August 1801.
12. *Ibid.*, p.48, 1707; p.90, 1724.
13. Third Governors' Order Book, Warwick CRO CR 1540/2, pp.88, 97, 104, 108, 162, 166; Warwick CRO CR 621/10-14, Book 18, f.142; and Warwick CRO CR 1540/1, pp.61, 168, 361 (1824, 1844, 1878).
14. Warwick CRO CR 1540/1, p.205 (1852), and p.462 (1888).
15. Warwick CRO CR Ba/52/1.
16. Tombstone in the nave of St Mary's Church has legend 'Mary the late wife of Thomas Evetts, died 9th June 1736 aged 49'.
17. Bills for 28 Dames' gowns: Warwick CRO W15/17/63H/13 and 43.
18. Warwick CRO CR 621/10-14, Copy Letter Books, 5 vols., 1919-27, 1931-33. Book 18, ff.95, 123, 151, 372, 376, 382, 385, 391, 401, 445; Warwick CRO CR 1540/2, p.184.

Chapter 15

1. Warwick CRO DR(B) 36/5 (not paginated).
2. Warwick CRO CR 1342/1, p.168 (1744).
3. *Ibid.*, pp.143, 153.
4. *Ibid.*, 4 August 1784 and 16 September 1790.
5. *Ibid.*, on a sheet stuck on the back of the front board of the first Governors' Order Book (date range 1688-1810).
6. G.M. Trevelyan, *English Social History* (1945), pp.191-2.
7. Warwick CRO CR 112/135/ Pt. I, indenture of 1683.

Chapter 16

1. A8/1670; Court of Arches, Lambeth Palace Library.
2. The probate inventory of Christopher's goods was appraised on 26 October 1669. The total value was the unusually large sum of £436. Warwick CRO. The original is now missing.
3. Warwick CRO DR (B) 36/5 Register of Dames.
4. Warwick CRO CR 112 Ba/53.
5. See Chapter 18 and Appendix IV.
6. P. Laslett, *The world we have lost* (1965), p.72 and note 79.

Chapter 17

1. Warwick CRO CR 1342/1, p.50 (1708).
2. Warwick CRO DR (B) 36/5.
3. Warwick CRO CR 1342/1, p.66 (1715).
4. *Ibid.*, p.74 (1720).
5. *Ibid.*, p.78 (1721); *VCH*, VIII, pp.431, 461, 508.
6. *Ibid.*, p.98 (1725), p.107 (1727), Smith's account for building the left side of the Hospital—£520 17s. 1d.
7. *Ibid.*, p.108 (1727).
8. *Ibid.*, p.234 (1771).

[9] There are a number of references to alterations to the two wings, one referred to as the 'assistant schoolmaster's house', the other as 'the matron's house', e.g. Warwick CRO CR 1540/1, p.104 (1834).

Chapter 18

[1] Warwick CRO CR 1342/1, p.138.
[2] Warwick CRO CR 1121/Ba 281; see note 2, Chapter 16.
[3] Warwick CRO CR 1342/1, pp.170, 222, 244; Warwick CRO DR(B) 36/1, vol.2.
[4] Ibid., p.134.
[5] Ibid., pp.141, 145; and see Appendix IV.
[6] Ibid., p.146.
[7] Ibid., p.150.
[8] Ibid., p.154.
[9] Ibid., p.158.
[10] Warwick CRO DR(B) 36/1, vol.2, p.1.
[11] By members of the Coventry and District Archaeological Society (CADAS) under the direction of Ray Wallwork. For a photograph of the group and their names see p.90.
[12] PRO E315/361, ff.15 to 20v. A copy is at Warwick CRO, CR/ Ba 188/2, f.24.
[13] For a full report of the finds, see Eileen Gooder, *Post-Medieval Archaeology*, 18 (1984), pp.149-249. A report of the archaeology of the excavation by Ray Wallwork is in Birmingham and Warwickshire Society, *Transactions*, vol.93, pp.57-72.
[14] Warwick CRO CR 621/6.
[15] R.C. Alvey, 'A Cesspit excavation at 26/28 High Pavement, Nottingham', in *Transactions of the Thoroton Society*, LXXVII (1973), 53 ff.
[16] I am indebted to Dr. Sandon, Curator of the Worcester Porcelain Museum, for this opinion.

Chapter 19

[1] Warwick CRO CR 1540/1, pp.99, 105.
[2] Ibid., pp.106 (January 1835), 108 (April 1835).
[3] Ibid., pp.109, 110, 111 (August 1835), 113 (January 1836).
[4] Ibid., pp.116, 118.
[5] Ibid., p.134.
[6] Ibid., pp.142-3, 152.

Chapter 20

[1] Warwick CRO CR 1540/1, pp.143-4, 146, 148.
[2] Ibid., p.158.
[3] Ibid., pp.163-4.
[4] Chapter 22.
[5] Ibid., p.166 (August 1845); Bailiff's Account Book in Bailiff's office, 1839-71; Warwick CRO CR 1540/1, p.333, 335, 343.
[6] Ibid., p.302.
[7] Ibid., pp.308, 313; Thomas Wedge's Map, Warwick CRO CR 621/8.

[8] Ibid., p.147; Bailiff's Account Book, 1839-71.
[9] Ibid., pp.143, 146.
[10] See e.g. G.M. Trevelyan, *English Social History* (1945), p.518.
[11] Warwick CRO CR 1540/1, pp.193-4.
[12] Ibid., p.204.
[13] Ibid., p.285 (1864).
[14] Ibid., p.277 (1862).
[15] Ibid., pp.268-70. For full details see Appendix IX
[16] Ibid., pp.252, 258.
[17] *VCH*, II (1947), p.370.
[18] Temple Balsall School Log Book (1863), Warwick CRO CR 3177/1. (Unfortunately no early log books for the girls have survived.)
[19] Warwick CRO CR 1540/1, p.302.
[20] Ibid., p.296.
[21] Ibid., pp.301-2; as has been described above, this was duly carried out.
[22] Ibid., pp.312, 321, and Warwick CRO CR 621/6, extract from Tomlinson's map of 1759.
[23] Ibid., p.143.
[24] Ibid., pp.318, 333, 343, 349, 359, 392.
[25] See Chapter 23.
[26] I am indebted to Mr Richard Lawton for allowing me to use this information from school log books in his possession.

Chapter 21

[1] Warwick CRO CR 1540/1, p.157.
[2] Ibid., p.164.
[3] *Dictionary of National Biography (Epitome)*, p.167; extract from Scott's report on St Mary's to the Governors, 16 January 1846, now in the Bailiff's office.
[4] Warwick CRO CR 1540/1, pp.169, 170, 172-3, 175.
[5] Ibid., p.177.
[6] Ibid., pp.180, 183-5.
[7] Ibid., pp.191, 194, 205, 209.
[8] Warwick CRO CR 1540/3/28.
[9] N. Pevsner and A. Wedgwood, *The Buildings of England, Warwickshire* (1966).
[10] Warwick CRO CR 1540/3/38.
[11] Warwick CRO CR 1540/3/20.
[12] Warwick CRO CR 1540/3/13, endorsed 'Blank plan of floor'; Bailiff's Account Book, 1839-71, in Bailiff's office, under 'Chapel Restoration Account, 1850, item 8, Minton for Encaustic tiles £106 7s 8d'.
[13] Warwick CRO T. Balsall Z1/74, Memorial Inscription in church and churchyard.
[14] Warwick CRO CR 1540/1, pp.410, 489, 496, 503.
[15] Cutting from unidentified local newspaper (1897) in the possession of Mr. Laurence Watts' family.
[16] Warwick CRO CR 1540/2, pp.59, 75, 80-1, 83, 85-6.
[17] Ibid., pp.95, 98-9, 107.
[18] The present Bailiff, Mr. Roger Stone, kindly loaned me the deed box.
[19] Warwick Library, Local History, *The Church of St*

Mary the Virgin ... at Temple Balsall in the County of Warwick, W726.5. Bailiff's Account Book at James and Lister Lea, Knowle, the present Bailiff's office.
20. Old Christmas card in the possession of Mr. Laurence Watts' family.
21. Warwick CRO CR 621/10-14, Copy Letter Books I, 1919-27, no18, f.44 (1919).
22. Lesley Jackson, ed., *Whitefriars Glass, The Art of James Powell and Sons,* catalogue produced to accompany an exhibition of their glass, Manchester City Art Galleries 27 January–30 June 1996 and Museum of London 30 July 1996–26 January 1997.
23. June Osborne, *Stained Glass in England* (Sutton Publishing, 1993).
24. Information from Mr. Geoffrey Burman, one of the Governors of the Lady Katherine Leveson Charity.
25. William Smith, *A New and Complete History of the County of Warwick,* Book 1, p.378; (quoted in Book 8, Temple Balsall Archive).

Chapter 22
1. Warwick CRO CR 40/1, p.211.
2. *Ibid.,* p.217.
3. *Ibid.,* p.213.
4. *Ibid.,* p.219.
5. *Ibid.,* p.223, 29 March 1856.
6. *Ibid.,* pp.228, 231, 232.
7. *Ibid.,* pp.255, 263, 275, 279-80.
8. *Ibid.,* p.285.
9. *Ibid.,* pp.304-5, 311.
10. Warwick CRO DR B/23/69/21.
11. Warwick CRO DR B/112/1, a small disintegrating scrapbook.
12. Information from the owners of St Richard's House.
13. Information from the present owners.
14. Warwick CRO DR B/23/67/19.
15. Temple Balsall Parochial Church Council (PCC) Minute Book 1948-1963.
16. Warwick CRO DR B/23/69/10 and 11; CR 1540/1, pp.304, 306.
17. Lady Katherine Leveson Charity Bailiff's Account Books, 1839-1871 and 1872-1886 (in the Bailiff's office).
18. Warwick CRO DR B/23/69/2, 4, 20; PCC Minute Book (*op.cit.*) 1955.
19. PCC Minute Book 1959, 1960.

Chapter 23
1. Bailiff's Account Book, 1872-1886, in present Bailiff's office; e.g. 1873, items 40, 45, 46 and 1881, items 40-44.
2. Warwick CRO CR 1540/1, p.401.
3. *Ibid.,* pp.372, 408, 410, 499.
4. *Ibid.,* p.424.

5. *Ibid.,* p.430.
6. Warwick CRO DR(B) 32/54; R. Lawton *et al, Balsall Parish Council, The First Hundred Years 1894-1994,* p.4.
7. *Ibid.,* pp.4-5.

Chapter 24
1. Warwick CRO CR 1540/1, p.441.
2. *Ibid.,* p.149 (1848).
3. *Ibid.,* p.442.
4. *Ibid.,* p.470.
5. *Ibid.,* pp.494, 524.
6. Warwick CRO CR 1540/2, pp.5, 41, 93, 103, 115, 130, 139-40, 159, 163.
7. Warwick CRO DR B/23/54, 6 May 1909; Copy Letter Book No.18, 15 February 1919–2 April 1921, f.24, and 6 May 1909.

Chapter 25
1. Warwick CRO CR 1540/1, p.61.
2. *Ibid.,* p.73, 1828.
3. See Chapter 14.
4. Warwick CRO CR 112/Ba/181 (unpaginated), 1783.
5. Information from Richard Chamberlain-Brother, archivist, Warwick County Record Office, to whom thanks.
6. E.g. Phyllis Deane and W.A. Cole, *British Economic Growth, 1688-1959,* 2nd edn (C.U.P., 1969), pp.12, 14; *VCH,* VII (1964), pp.279-83.
7. Warwick CRO CR 112/Ba/181 (unpaginated), 1806.
8. *Ibid.,* 1806.
9. *Ibid.,* 1806.
10. Warwick CRO CR 1540/1, p.429.
11. See Chapter 14, and Warwick CRO CR 621/1, Register of Candidates, pp.22 *et seq.*—this volume would repay further study; The Office for National Statistics (HMSO), *Mortality Statistics* (1993-5), Table 46. I am indebted to Dr. D. Sheppard for these figures.
12. Robert Woods, *The Population of Britain in the Nineteenth Century* (C.U.P., 1995), p.17. I am indebted to Dr. P. Searby for this reference.
13. Warwick CRO DR B23/54, no.18, f.203.

Appendix IV
1. Christopher's inventory cannot now be found. Hearth Tax records—Warwick CRO QS/11/4, 5, 20, 32, 45, 59, and CRO Z336/1 and 2.
2. Warwick CRO CR 112/177/1.
3. Warwick CRO QS/11/32.
4. Francis' inventory Warwick CRO CR 112/Ba65/21; Margaret's *ibid.* /41.
5. Gooder, p.66.
6. *Ibid.,* Fig.29 and caption.

Bibliography

Bennett, H.S., *Life on the English Manor, 1150-1400* (Cambridge University Press, 1960)

Coulton, G.G., *The Medieval Village* (Cambridge University Press, 1925)

Deane, Phyllis and Cole, N.A., *British Economic Growth 1688-1959* (Cambridge University Press, 2nd edn, 1969)

Humphery-Smith, C., *Hugh Revel* (Phillimore, 1994)

Jackson, Lesley (ed.), *Whitefriars Glass* (1996)

Kendall, A., *Robert Dudley, Earl of Leicester* (1980)

King, Edwin, *The Knights of St John in the British Empire* (1934)

Larking & Kemble, *The Knights Hospitallers in England, The Report of Philip de Thame ... 1338*, Camden Society, vol.LXV (1858)

Laslett, P., *The World We Have Lost* (1965)

McKisack, May, *The Fourteenth Century* (Oxford, 1959)

Nicholson, H., *Templars, Hospitallers and Teutonic Knights* (1995)

Osborne, June, *Stained Glass in England* (1981)

Pevsner, N. and Wedgwood, A., *The Buildings of England, Warwickshire* (1966)

Riley-Smith, J., *The Knights of St John in Jerusalem and Cyprus, 1050-1310* (1967)

Salzman, L.F., *Building in England down to 1540* (Oxford University Press, 1952)

Titow, J.Z., *English Rural Society, 1200-1350* (1969)

Trevelyan, G.M., *A Social History of England* (1942)

Victoria History of the County of Warwick, vol.II (William Page, ed.) (1908); vol.III (Philip Styles, ed.) (1945); vol.IV (L.F. Salzman, ed.) (1947)

Woods, Robert, *The Population of Britain in the Nineteenth Century* (Cambridge University Press, 1995)

Index